Hillary Clinton
To
Destroy A Nation

Will Clark

Hillary Clinton
To
Destroy a Nation

ISBN-13: 978-1536855708

ISBN-10: 1536855707

Published By
Motivation Basics
P.O. Box 6327
Diamondhead, MS 39525

Will01@aol.com

For more information visit the author at:

AuthorsDen.com

QUOTE

"A nation can survive its fools, and even the ambitious. But it cannot survive treason from within. An enemy at the gates is less formidable, for he is known and carries his banner openly. But the traitor moves amongst those within the gate freely, his sly whispers rustling through all the alleys, heard in the very halls of government itself. For the traitor appears not a traitor; he speaks in accents familiar to his victims, and he wears their face and their arguments, he appeals to the baseness that lies deep in the hearts of all men. He rots the soul of a nation, he works secretly and unknown in the night to undermine the pillars of the city, he infects the body politic so that it can no longer resist. A murderer is less to fear. The traitor is the plague." *Marcus Tullius Cicero, 58 B.C. Speech in the Roman Senate*

QUOTE

"Throughout recorded time, and probably since the end of the Neolithic Age, there have been three kinds of people in the world, the High, the Middle, and the Low. They have been subdivided in many ways, they have borne countless different names, and their relative numbers, as well as their attitude towards one another, have varied from age to age: but the essential structure of society has never altered. Even after enormous upheavals and seemingly irrevocable changes, the same pattern has always reasserted itself, just as a gyroscope will always return to equilibrium, however far it is pushed one way or the other --

.

'Julia, are you awake?' said Winston.

'Yes, my love, I'm listening. Go on. It's marvellous.'

He continued reading:

The aims of these three groups are entirely irreconcilable. The aim of the High is to remain where they are. The aim of the Middle is to change places with the High. The aim of the Low, when they have an aim -- for it is an abiding characteristic of the Low that they are too much crushed by drudgery to be more than intermittently conscious of anything outside their daily lives -- is to abolish all distinctions and create a society in which all men shall be equal. Thus throughout history a struggle which is the same in its main outlines recurs over and over again. For long periods the High seem to be securely in power, but sooner or later there always comes a moment when they lose either their belief in themselves or their capacity to govern efficiently, or both. They are then overthrown by the Middle, who enlist the Low on their side by pretending to them that they are fighting for liberty and justice. As soon as they have reached their objective, the Middle thrust the Low back into their old position of servitude, and themselves become the High. Presently a new Middle group splits off from one of the other groups, or from both of them, and the struggle begins over again. Of the three groups, only the Low are never even temporarily successful in achieving their aims. It would be an exaggeration to say that throughout history there has been no progress of a material kind. Even today, in a period of decline, the average human being is physically better off than he was a few centuries ago. But no advance in wealth, no softening of manners, no reform or revolution has ever brought human equality a millimetre nearer. From the point of view of the Low, no historic change has ever meant much more than a change in the name of their masters."

(From the novel, 1984, by George Orwell. This quote is from an old book Winston found. He is reading to his girlfriend, Julia, as they meet in their temporary meeting place, thinking they are hidden from Big Brother. Winston is reading from Chapter 1, titled: Ignorance is Strength.)

Contents

Introduction

Pandora's box has been opened wide in our current politically correct society. The box has been opened and evil has spilled out all across our nation and our world. For the many who don't know about 'Pandora's Box' this is a brief description from Wikipedia:

"Pandora's box is an artifact in Greek mythology, taken from the myth of Pandora's creation in Hesiod's Works and Days. The "box" was actually a large jar given to Pandora which contained all the evils of the world. Pandora opened the jar and all the evils flew out, leaving only "Hope" inside once she had closed it again.

Today the phrase "to open Pandora's box" means to perform an action that may seem small or innocent, but that turns out to have severely detrimental and far-reaching negative consequences."

In a January 16, 1991 speech, George Bush the elder identified the opportunity to build a New World Order, "where the rule of law… governs the conduct of nations," and "in which a credible United Nations can use its peacekeeping role to fulfill the promise and vision of the UN's founders."

This term, 'New World Order' in his speech has been interpreted to mean several and different things. But, the most significant meaning is that we might have a 'New World Order' which is guided by one all-powerful government. If that's the case and if that's the real meaning; then the concept of that term invites many dangers for our great nation. It implies that our nation should be the same as all other nations. This has been the mantra of Barack Obama during his term in office; and it seems to be the same goal of Hillary Clinton if she succeeds in becoming president of the United States. There are key words that reveal the subtle and shaded attempts to accomplish this goal.

The first attempt was under the banner of 'Agenda 21.' That hidden agenda of Agenda 21 was quickly uncovered, so a new banner emerged. That banner was 'Sustainable Development.' When that concept lost its hold the words were changed again to give itself more credibility and to sustain its mission of creating a one-world government. The new banner became 'Global Warming.' When that was challenged, the new and current mantra became, 'Climate Change.'

Do not be fooled or mislead. No matter the name of the monster, the goal of the term is to create a one-world government.

Now, perhaps there really is a warming of our world. For either side of the argument to hold fast to their ideology is a wasted effort; for there has been climate change before and after the great Ice Age. Only a few people existed on earth at that time; certainly they could not have contributed to global warming with their few campfires. And, that's after they discovered fire. In all likelihood, more global warning, climate change, was created by lightening fires and volcanic eruptions than by those campfires. Possibly the same exists today; we still have lightening fires and volcanic eruptions. In reality, everything contributes in some degree to global warming. Most however, likely is not significantly controllable by man's actions or inactions.

Keep in mind, however, as you read the following information that controlling climate and emissions has nothing to do with the purpose for the demand for taking actions to reduce carbon emissions. It has everything to do with creating a one-world order; under the pretense of reducing global warming. Our world leaders, who see their power increasing under these new Agenda 21 programs, have opened 'Pandora's Box.' We have invited Islam in, through the back door, to establish their own interpretation of the New World Order under strict Islamic Sharia codes. Maybe Agenda 21 concepts would not have been so bad after all, comparing it to the murderous results of Islam.

How have they been invited to slip in through the back door to terrorize the world? In the global leaders' efforts to make the world one, they are ignoring human movement throughout the world. Although most nations have immigration laws, those trying to impose the new world order encourage humans to integrate economically and socially throughout the world. Therefore, little is done to filter out those Muslims flowing past once important borders that are now ignored by design. When levels of Muslim integration reaches certain levels then their religious zealotry springs from their beings to control and destroy those who are not of them. Their evil then cannot be forced back into Pandora's box. The next chapter will explain that Muslim evolution as the percentage of immigration changes.

Those Islamic ideologies alone are not the single greatest threat to our nation. That great threat is combined with another to create confusion; and to eliminate a clear target at which to take our aim. That other great danger is the ideology of Saul Alinsky followed by Barack Obama and Hillary Clinton.

There is a clear association, a linchpin, between Barack Obama and Hillary Clinton. That connection, that association of ideologies is grounded in the works of a man named Saul Alinsky. The following is an article at Discoverthenetworks.org that introduces that connection. The article is titled, Barack Obama's Unlikely Political Education. It's subtitled, 'The Agitator.' The article is presented by Ryan Lizza, 3-9-07. This is an extract from that article:

"In 1985, Barack Obama traveled halfway across the country to take a job that he didn't fully understand. But, while he knew little about his new vocation--community organizer it still had a romantic ring, at least to his 24-year-old ears. With his old classmates from Columbia, he had talked frequently about political change. Now, he was moving to Chicago to put that talk into action. His 1995 memoir, Dreams from My Father, recounts his idealistic effusions: "Change won't come from the top, I would say. Change will come from a mobilized grass roots. That's what I'll do. I'll organize black folks. At the grass roots. for change."

His excitement wasn't rooted merely in youthful enthusiasm but also in the psychology of a vagabond. By 1985, Obama had already lived in Hawaii, where he was born and raised by his white mother and grandparents; Indonesia, where he lived briefly as a child; Los Angeles, where he started college; and New York, where he finished it. After these itinerant years, he would finally be able to insinuate himself into a community--and not just any community, but, as he later put it, "the capital of the African American community in the country." Every strain of black political thought seemed to converge in Chicago in the1980s.

It was the intellectual center of Black Nationalism, the base both for Jesse Jackson's presidential campaigns and for Louis Farrakhan's Nation of Islam. Moreover, on the eve of Obama's arrival, Harold Washington had overthrown Richard J. Daley's white ethnic machine to become the city's first black mayor. It was, in short, an ideal place for an identity-starved Kenyan Kansan to immerse himself in a more typical black American experience.

Not long after Obama arrived, he sat down for a cup of coffee in Hyde Park with a fellow organizer named Mike Kruglik. Obama's work focused on helping poor blacks on Chicago's South Side fight the city for things like job banks and asbestos removal. His teachers were schooled in a style of organizing devised by Saul Alinsky, the radical University of Chicago trained social scientist. At the heart of the Alinsky method is the concept of "agitation"--making someone angry enough about the rotten state of his life that he agrees to take action to change it; or, as Alinsky himself described the job, to "rub raw the sores of discontent."

In Dreams, Obama spent some 150 pages on his four years in Chicago working as an organizer, but there's little discussion of the theory that undergirded his work and informed that of his teachers. Alinsky is the missing layer of his account.

Born in 1909 to Russian-Jewish immigrants, Alinsky had prowled the same neighborhoods that Obama now worked and internalized many of the same lessons. As a University of Chicago criminology graduate student, he ingratiated himself with Al Capone's mobsters to learn all he could about the dynamics of the city's underworld, an experience that helped foster a lifelong appreciation for seeing the world as it actually exists, rather than through the academic's idealized prism. Charming and self-absorbed, Alinsky would entertain friends with stories--some true, many embellished--from his mob days for decades afterward. He was profane, outspoken, and narcissistic, always the center of attention despite his tweedy, academic look and thick, horn-rimmed glasses.

Alinsky was deeply influenced by the great social science insight of his times, one developed by his professors at Chicago: that the pathologies of the urban poor were not hereditary but environmental. This idea, that people could change their lives by changing their surroundings, led him to take an obscure social science phrase--"the community organization"--and turn it into, in the words of Alinsky biographer Sanford Horwitt, "something controversial, important, even romantic." His starting point was an early fascination with John L. Lewis, the great labor leader and founder of the CIO. What if, Alinsky wondered, the same hardheaded tactics used by unions could be applied to the relationship between citizens and public officials?

To test his theory, Alinsky left the world of academia in the 1930s and set up shop in Chicago's meatpacking neighborhood, the "Back of the Yards"--the same wretched, multiethnic enclave that Upton Sinclair had chronicled three decades earlier in The Jungle. He created the Back of the Yards Neighborhood Council, which won a succession of victories against businesses and decreased crime, while increasing cooperation between rival ethnic groups. The results were impressive enough that they were celebrated far beyond Chicago in newspaper stories with headlines like, "they called him a 'red,' but young sociologist did the job."

Alinsky had been dead for more than a decade when Obama arrived in Chicago, but his legacy was still very much alive. Kruglik, Kellman, and Galluzzo had all studied his teachings through the Industrial Areas Foundation (IAF), the organizing school Alinsky founded. By the '80s, not even the IAF strictly adhered to every principle that Alinsky taught. But at least one of Obama's teachers considered himself a true believer: "I regard myself as St. Paul who never met Jesus," Galluzzo told me of Alinsky, who died shortly after Galluzzo moved to Chicago on a pilgrimage to meet him in 1972. "I'm his best disciple." Alinsky has attracted other, more famous admirers, including Hillary Clinton, who wrote an undergraduate thesis about him, a favorite bit of trivia for right-wingers.

But, while Alinsky is often viewed as an ideological figure--toward the end of his life, New Left radicals tried to claim him as one of their own--to place Alinsky within a taxonomy of left-wing politics is to miss the point. His legacy is less ideological than methodological. Alinsky's contribution to community organizing was to create a set of rules, a clear-eyed and systemic approach that ordinary citizens can use to gain public power. The first and most fundamental lesson Obama learned was to reassess his understanding of power. Horwitt says that, when Alinsky would ask new students why they wanted to organize, they would invariably respond with selfless bromides about wanting to help others. Alinsky would then scream back at them that there was a one-word answer: "You want to organize for power!" End of article.

Two important conclusions should be made from this article. First, Barack Obama's actions have been to follow Alinsky's guidelines to disrupt and destroy the influence of our responsible national leaders; simply to destroy, not to build something better. Second, Hillary Clinton leans strongly toward that same ideology; to destroy 'what is' not to replace it with something better. They both are endowed with that Alinsky fever. We will consider those Alinsky ideologies she represents in a later chapter.

Chapter 1
Peace that Destroys

W hat is Hillary Clinton's answer to the question, 'how many Muslims should we allow into our great nation?' If history is any predictor, her answer would likely be, 'What difference does it make.'

Hillary Clinton Recently said on Face the Nation at CBS, "I would like to see us move from what is a good start, 10,000, to 65,000." In that statement, she proposes bringing in at least 65,000 and even more Syrian refugees into our nation. Does she recognize the danger; does she care? Maybe her answer would be, 'What difference does it make?'

Well, in fact, the percentage of Muslims in any nation does make a great difference. When the numbers get large enough, that once free nation is no longer free. This is understood by recognizing the four 'stages of Islamization.' This link is only one of the many that expose this Islamic take-over process to create Sharia everywhere and for everyone:

http://www.siotw.org/news_english.item.607/these-are-the-steps-of-islamization.html

"These are the steps of Islamization:

Stage I of Islamic Conquests begins with Infiltration.

Migration: Muslims have migrated to America en masse, as they have in Europe. There are already pockets of neighborhoods in which they live apart from others, intentionally establishing their isolation with exclusively Muslim schools. Previous waves of immigrants brought people who eagerly assimilated to become proud Americans.

Appeal for Humanitarian tolerance: From severely intolerant lands, they begin their appeal for tolerance. America had already learned to accept the "tired, the poor, the huddled masses yearning to breathe free." The "melting pot" welcomed new immigrants who lived adjacent to and among each other, and the children became Americans together. But the Muslim strategy is to demand special privileges, such as inviting the Muslim Brotherhood-affiliate, Muslim Student Union, into a Catholic-University, rather than assimilate or attend secular schools, to break down the existing system.

Revise history: Muslims attempt to portray Islam as a religion of peace, and the Muslims as victims of misunderstanding or racism (they're not a race). History books are revised in America so as to secrete Islam's true jihadist history, just as Muslims have built mosques over razed churches, synagogues and temples to eliminate them from memory.

High Muslim birthrate is encouraged in host countries to increase Muslim population The US Muslim population increased greatly in the 20th century, due to rising immigration and conversion, and a comparatively high birth rate. In 2005, nearly 96,000 people from Islamic countries became legal permanent United States residents than in any previous year.

Mosques are used to spread hate of the host country and culture. There are more than 2,000 mosques in America, and Muslims, led by Imam Rauf, are working hard to use our laws to establish a caliphate, by constructing a rabat-style mosque of conquest on Ground Zero, designed to house a war room, resting places for jihadists, and not one with the typically round configuration for prayer. Rauf also threatened that if he did not build his mosque there, "the Islamists might get violent."

Islamophobia: Threats of Islamophobia, already prevalent, are used as a means of controlling our speech. Citizens are discouraged/forbidden from mentioning certain words for fear of offending — not identifying terrorists, no media attention to jihad attacks worldwide or local. Our media has failed to alert us to the 17,000+ jihadist attacks worldwide since 9/11, including the numerous Christian villages burned to the ground, the Muslims who attacked and carved a Star of David into the back of a pro-Israel Iraqi poet in St. Louis, or the US universities that do little to discourage hate crimes on campus. Now CAIR (Council on American-Islamic Relations) and the Muslim Brotherhood are in control of what our media may announce/write, and the Obama administration is pulling back all training manuals used for law enforcement material and national security that refer to Islam, deemed offensive to Muslims, thereby eliminating the ability to name those who endanger our national security. (This is exemplified as 'Oldspeak' and 'Newspeak' in George Orwell's novel, '1984.'

Lawfare: Threats of legal action for perceived discrimination, to criminalize honest discussion on Islamic texts and teachings of violence — using libel and defamation laws as weapons to intimidate democracy into silence. And the publisher who bowed to threats, did not produce his book that contained cartoons about Muhammad.

Offers of interfaith dialogue to indoctrinate non-Muslims. These are perceived by many to be a form of outreach, such as reported by Nathan Guttman. However, one of the rabbis in attendance was Rabbi Eric Yoffie, past-president of the Union for Reform Judaism, a branch that has been known to affiliate with J Street, whose solutions for peace are considered by most Israelis to be suicidal. They purport to speak for most American Jews, and claim to be pro-Israel, yet they receive their financial support from George Soros, pro-Palestinians, pro-Iranians, and have never taken a pro-Israel position on anything.

The next stages of the Islamization of America would be:

Stage 2: Consolidation of Power

Stage 3: Open war with Leadership and Culture

Stage 4: Totalitarianism, Islamic 'theocracy' and the full implementation of Sharia.

So what is it about this kind of conquest that journalists fail to understand? What will it take for the media and many of our population to acknowledge that Stage 2 is at hand?" End of Article.

But in 'Hillary thinking;' 'What difference does it make?' While Islamic terrorists wreak havoc and behead people across the world; why should we worry if a few come into our great nation to kill more of us. In Hillarythink, as Orwell might express; it's okay to lose a few good Americans as long as the world is assimilated together as one. And, more keep rushing in at the invitation of Barack Obama, and soon Hillary Clinton.

Can you believe Hillary would make a statement like this, while at the same time blaming police for horrible interactions between police and African Americans? Which or whose side is she on anyway? Her comments have nothing to do with honor or honesty; only what she thinks advances her determined political agenda. Rationality, honor, nor the love of America has any place in her heart for her comments or actions; only treachery and dishonor. This is that comment via

Breitbart:

"Democratic presidential front-runner Hillary Clinton said Monday that blocking Syrian refugees from entering the United States would impair the ability of police officers to connect with the Muslim community.

Clinton, who wants to import thousands of Syrian refugees, told reporters in Reno that it would look bad not to let in Syrian refugees, and that might inflame Muslims against law enforcement. What rational patriotic American would ever imagine or make such an irrational statement such as this?

"If you're in law enforcement ... you want the people in the communities that you are looking to get information from to feel like they want to help you," Clinton said at a Nevada roundtable. "And if the message from people who are running for president, for example, is that we don't want to take any Muslims whatsoever, that's not good for law enforcement." This is the link to that statement:

http://www.weaselzippers.us/241604-hillary-clinton-muslim-refugees-will-be-mad-at-law-enforcement-if-we-dont-let-them-in/

Although Muslims claim to be 'peaceful' and are members of a 'religion of peace' their peaceful actions depend upon the percentage of Muslims in the population of a country. The higher the percentage of Muslims, the less peace is allowed in that population. This is an article titled, 'How Islam Manifest based on Percentage Muslim Population,' submitted by Edward Cline as reported at this link:

https://balaamsarse.wordpress.com/2011/11/01/how-islam-manifests-based-on-percentage-muslim-population/

"In remembrance of those who died 10 years ago on the 11th of

September 2001 – a time when Islam declared its full hand and its ultimate intention for the non-Islamic West.

As I often discuss the impact of Islam, and particularly Islamic immigration, upon Western nations on this blog, I thought it may be worthwhile citing material which details the typical impact of Islam on the host nation based on Muslim population as a percentage of the greater whole. I have shortened the main article and highlighted the Muslim percentage makeup of the various nations cited. For the complete article please refer to the following link above. The original article is titled, 'Jihad by the Numbers.'

It is no accident or fluke of history that Islamists – Hamas, Hezbollah, Ahmadinejad, Saudi Wahhabists, the whole ménage of Islamists and Jihadists — admire both Hitler and Nazism. Their hatred of Jews and Israel is merely one facet of that pathology. As Nazism required the complete submission of the individual to Party ideology and an unthinking, unwavering deference to Hitler, Islam requires the complete submission of the individual to Islam and an unthinking, unwavering deference to Allah and Mohammed. Islamists have long recognized that both the method and the ends of Nazism were in complete agreement and practical accord with their own. The "mechanics" of a functioning Islam differ in no fundamental way from the "mechanics" of a functioning Nazism or any other brand of total collectivism.

With that in mind, here is a set of significant statistics forwarded to me by a friend. It charts the progression of Islamic Jihad, both soft and hard methods, whose purpose is to establish a global caliphate, especially in the West.

It begins by stating: "Islam is not a religion nor is it a cult. It is a complete system."

I would disagree. It is definitely a religion and a political system combined. Any attempt to "separate" mosque and state would emasculate Islam. I have argued this point in past commentaries and will not dwell on it here. And cults, if not opposed by reason and kept by it on the far fringes of a civilized society, have a tendency to become religions that may become state policies. Ecology was once a "cult." Today we have the Environmental Protection Agency.

It goes on to state: "Islam has religious, legal, political, economic and military components. The religious component is a beard for all the other components."

Or a mask, or a ruse. But no one should doubt how seriously Islamists and Muslims in general take the religious component. Islam is a barbaric but fully integrated system, perhaps more lethally integrated than was Nazism. "Islamization occurs when there are sufficient Muslims in a country to agitate for their so-called 'religious rights.'"

I would defend anyone's right to believe in Islam. The question is: How could one truly practice Islam without declaring Jihad on others? After a Muslim has won the "internal struggle" or Jihad within himself, the next step is to wage it against all others. To refrain from that part of Jihad is to risk the accusation of being a slacker or pseudo-Muslim. From the first stage to the last, all such effort constitutes "working towards the Prophet and Allah."

"When politically correct and culturally diverse societies agreed to 'the reasonable' Muslims demands for their 'religious rights,' they also get the other components under the table. Here's how it works (percentages source: CIA: The World Fact Book, 2007).

(Before we begin this analysis, please keep in mind that this 'dangerous peace' is identified in the Bible at Daniel 8:25: "And through his policy also he shall cause craft to prosper in his hand; and he shall magnify himself in his heart, and by peace shall destroy many." Therefore, Muslims with their 'Religion of Peace' are destroying many. This analysis continues at one percent):

One Percent: "As long as the Muslim population remains around 1% of any given country it will be regarded as a peace-loving minority and not as a threat to anyone...." Here is where it becomes interesting. Note throughout the exponential scale of Islamic influence as the percentage of Muslim population per country increases. Comments in square brackets are my corrective interjections.

United States: 1.0
Australia: 1.5
Canada: 1.9
China: 1.0-2.0
Italy: 1.5
Norway: 1.8

Two to Three Percent: "At 2% and 3% they [Muslims] begin to proselytize from other ethnic minorities and disaffected groups with major recruiting from the jails and among street gangs."

Denmark: 2.0
Germany: 3.7
United Kingdom: 2.7
Spain: 4.0
Italy: 4.6

Five Percent and Over: "From 5% on they [Muslims] exercise an inordinate influence in proportion to their percentage of the population. They will push for the introduction of halal ("clean" by Islamic standards) food, thereby securing food preparation jobs for Muslims. They will increase pressure on supermarket chains to feature it on their shelves – along with threats for failure to comply (United States)."

France: 8.0
Philippines: 5.0
Sweden: 5.0
Switzerland: 4.3
The Netherlands: 5.5
Trinidad & Tobago: 5.8

At this point, they [Muslims] will work to get the ruling government to allow them to rule themselves under Sharia, or Islamic law. The ultimate goal of Islam is not to convert the world but to establish Sharia law over the entire world.

Ten Percent and Over: "When Muslims reach 10% of the population, they will increase lawlessness as a means of complaint about their conditions (Paris – car burning). Any non-Muslim action that offends Islam will result in uprisings and threats (Amsterdam, Denmark – Mohammed cartoons, murder of Theo van Gogh)."

Guyana: 10.0
India: 13.4
Israel: 16.0
Kenya: 10.0
Russia: 10.0-15.0

The one anomaly in this set of statistics is Israel, which has not experienced uprisings and threats of violence. Its Arab or Muslim population enjoys equal political rights with Jewish Israelis. The suicide bombings and rocket attacks that have killed hundreds have been perpetrated by outsiders.

Twenty Percent and Over: "After reaching 20% [of a population] expect hair-trigger rioting, Jihad militia formations, sporadic killings and church and synagogue burning:"

Ethiopia: 32.8

Forty Percent and Over: "After 40% you will find widespread massacres, chronic terror attacks and ongoing militia warfare:"

Bosnia: 40.0
Chad: 53.1
Lebanon: 59.7

Sixty Percent and Over: "From 60% you may expect unfettered persecution of non-believers and other religions, sporadic ethnic cleansing (genocide), use of Sharia Law as a weapon and jizya, the tax placed on [conquered] infidels:"

Albania: 70.0
Malaysia: 60.4
Qatar: 77.5
Sudan: 70.0"

Eighty Percent and Over: "After 80%, expect state-run ethnic cleansing and genocide:"

Bangladesh: 83.0
Egypt: 90.0
Gaza: 98.7
Indonesia: 86.1
Iran: 98.0
Iraq: 97.0
Jordan: 92.0
Morocco: 98.7
Pakistan: 97.0

Palestine: 99.0
Syria: 90.0
Tajikistan: 90.0
Turkey: 99.8
United Arab Emirates: 96.0

I question the inclusion of "Palestine" in this set. "Palestine" simply means space occupied by stateless "Palestinians" in Gaza and the West Bank, and is the name of the state which Islamists wish to replace Israel, once it is destroyed. Turkey, after decades of having a secular, non-religious government, is beginning to turn "religious," and seems to be yearning for the kind of Muslim government that cleansed the country in 1915 of non-Muslim Armenians in a genocide that predates the Holocaust.

One Hundred Percent: "100% will usher in the peace of 'Dar-es-Salaam' – the Islamic House of Peace' [more correctly, dar-al-Islam, or Land of Islam]. There is supposed to be peace because everybody is a Muslim."

Afghanistan: 100.0
Saudi Arabia: 100.0
Somalia: 100.0
Yemen: 99.9

"Of course, that's not the case. To satisfy their blood lust, Muslims then start killing each other for a variety of reasons. 'Before I was nine I had learned the basic canon of Arab life. It was me against my brother; me and my brother against our father; my family against my cousins and the clan; the clan against the tribe; and the tribe against the world and all of us against the infidel.' Leon Uris, The Haj."

(Author's Note: This blood lust of Muslims killing one another is described in Revelation 6:3-4, "And when he had opened the second seal, I heard the second beast say, Come and see. And there went out another horse that was red: and power was given to him that sat thereon to take peace from the earth, and that they should kill one another: and there was given unto him a great sword." This one rider describes Islam. When Muslims have no one else to kill they 'kill one another.')

"It is good to remember that in many, many countries, such as France, the Muslim populations are centered around ghettos based on their ethnicity. Muslims do not integrate into the community at large. Therefore, they exercise more power than their national average[s] would indicate."

"Adapted from Dr. Peter Hammond's book, Slavery, Terrorism and Islam: The Historical Roots and Contemporary Threat." End of Article.

So, in conclusion, should we invite Muslims, who worship Satan, into our great nation, founded on Christian principles? Christ answers this question in 2 John, 9-11:

"Whosoever transgresseth, and abideth not in the doctrine of Christ, hath not God. He that abideth in the doctrine of Christ, he hath both the Father and the Son. If there come any unto you, and bring not this doctrine, receive him not into your house, and neither bid him God speed. For he that biddeth him God speed is partaker of his evil deeds."

Muslims refute the idea that Jesus Christ is the Son of God. They consider Jesus a subservient prophet below Muhammad. Therefore, in God's words; we must not allow them into our nation to destroy us and our 'One nation under God with liberty and justice for all.'

Too many Muslims have already been allowed into too many other

28

countries, in good faith; and now they are already destroying those once great nations. The destruction will not end; it's their ultimate plan. It's Satan's plan that for God in heaven "that there should be time no longer." (Revelation 10: 5-6)

Why is Barack Obama rushing so many ungodly Muslims into America? We know the answer to this question. But, why does Hillary Clinton plan to bring in even more? She's not a Muslim; so why should she be in such defiance of God's warning to 'receive them not into our house?'

Chapter 2
The Silent Jihad

B arack Obama's administration began with lies and deceit. Perhaps that started even before Obama was elected President of the United States. Although he produced a birth certificate indicating he was born in Hawaii; he still hasn't produced explanations for a questionable social security number, and he refuses to release his school records to prove he wasn't registered as a foreign student. And, he has all along claimed to be a Christian, but all his actions, suggestions, and support have been indications of an Islamic foundation. His first clearly self-evident deception, however, was his claim that 'If you like your doctor, you can keep your doctor.' Events after that statement clearly show that was a deceptive promise. His full term has been guided by lies, deceptions, falsehoods, and even blasphemy against God. His only praises are to Islam – and himself.

He strives with every effort to allow more Muslims into our peaceful nation. He has expressed no concern whether or not they are 'peaceful' or terrorists. He just wants them here to increase their numbers and influence in America. One must ask; why? Anyone who understands anything about the 'plan' of the Muslim Brotherhood will know that answer. Their written plan is to conquer America and the Western World by a process they identify as 'Settlement.' If and when that occurs, no true American will be safe. Christians must then become Muslim or become beheaded. That's their plan; and Obama expresses no words or actions to discourage or thwart that plan. The question has even been proposed to question his being part of that plan, as a hidden member of that Brotherhood. It may be read at this link, and others:

content/uploads/2014/05/Explanatory_Memoradum.pdf

So, how is Hillary Clinton related to this subversive plan? That answer will be given later in this book, but for now let's introduce that dangerous and subversive plan to understand why Obama is so anxious to facilitate its full implementation; as he has so well done during his administration to *'serve the American people?'* The link above gives the full information. It's presented in both, Arabic and English.

This attack on the United States and Christians is from a concept called the 'Third Jihad,' often called the 'Silent Jihad.' In this effort, Muslims have a long-range plan to transpose America into a total Islamic country "without firing a single shot." It's from a Muslim Brotherhood plan discovered in 1991, titled, 'An Explanatory Memorandum: On the General Strategic Goal for the Group In North America.' Just take a casual look around and you will see how far they have already progressed in this effort. Many Islamists (connected to the Muslim Brotherhood) are already in powerful positions in our government - including important advisory positions to the President of the United States.

The direct and bloody Islamic jihad against America and all Western civilizations, that anyone who doesn't comply with radical Islamic ideology will be killed, is not the only Islamic war to control the United States and the rest of the world. There is also a more insidious plan to accomplish that ideological goal silently from within. Their plan is already well advanced in the United States. Many citizens know about it, but nothing is done to stop it. Barack Obama and his supporters seem to be facilitating this Islamic goal. This article at the link above is from Discoverthenetworks.org. It gives an overview:

"In July 2007, seven key leaders of an Islamic charity known as the Holy Land Foundation for Relief and Development (HLF) went on trial for charges that they had: (a) provided "material support and resources" to a foreign terrorist organization (namely Hamas); (b) engaged in money laundering; and (c) breached the International Emergency Economic Powers Act, which prohibits transactions that threaten American national security. Along with the seven named defendants, the U.S. government released a list of approximately 300 "unindicted co-conspirators" and "joint venturers." During the course of the HLF trial, many incriminating documents were entered into evidence. Perhaps the most significant of these was "An Explanatory Memorandum on the General Strategic Goal for the Group in North America," by the Muslim Brotherhood operative Mohamed Akram. Federal investigators found Akram's memo in the home of Ismael Elbarasse, a founder of the Dar Al-Hijrah mosque in Falls Church, Virginia, during a 2004 search. Elbarasse was a member of the Palestine Committee, which the Muslim Brotherhood had created to support Hamas in the United States.

Written sometime in 1987 but not formally published until May 22, 1991, Akram's 18-page document listed the Brotherhood's 29 likeminded "organizations of our friends" that shared the common goal of dismantling American institutions and turning the U.S. into a Muslim nation. These "friends" were identified by Akram and the Brotherhood as groups that could help convince Muslims "that their work in America is a kind of grand Jihad in eliminating and destroying the Western civilization from within and 'sabotaging' its miserable house by their hands ... so that ... God's religion [Islam] is made victorious over all other religions."

Akram was well aware that in the U.S., it would be extremely difficult to promote Islam by means of terror attacks. Thus the "grand jihad" that he and his Brotherhood comrades envisioned was not a violent one involving bombings and shootings, but rather a stealth (or "soft") jihad aiming to impose Islamic law (Sharia) over every region of the earth by incremental, non-confrontational means, such as working to "expand the observant Muslim base"; to "unif[y] and direc[t] Muslims' efforts"; and to "present Islam as a civilization alternative." At its heart, Akram's document details a plan to conquer and Islamize the United States – not as an ultimate objective, but merely as a stepping stone toward the larger goal of one day creating "the global Islamic state."

In line with this objective, Akram and the Brotherhood resolved to "settle" Islam and the Islamic movement within the United States, so that the Muslim religion could be "enabled within the souls, minds and the lives of the people of the country." Akram explained that this could be accomplished "through the establishment of firmly-rooted organizations on whose bases civilization, structure and testimony are built." He urged Muslim leaders to make "a shift from the collision mentality to the absorption mentality," meaning that they should abandon any tactics involving defiance or confrontation, and seek instead to implant into the larger society a host of seemingly benign Islamic groups with ostensibly unobjectionable motives; once those groups had gained a measure of public acceptance, they would be in a position to more effectively promote societal transformation by the old Communist technique of "boring from within."

"The heart and the core" of this strategy, said Akram, was contingent upon these groups' ability to develop "a mastery of the art of 'coalitions.'" That is, by working synergistically they could complement, augment, and amplify one another's efforts. Added Akram: "The big challenge that is ahead of us is how to turn these seeds or 'scattered' elements into comprehensive, stable, 'settled' organizations that are connected with our Movement and which fly in our orbit and take orders from our guidance." The ultimate objective was not only an enlarged Muslim presence, but also implementation of the Brotherhood objectives of transforming pluralistic societies, particularly America, into Islamic states, and sweeping away Western notions of legal equality, freedom of conscience, freedom of religion, and freedom of speech.

Akram and the Brotherhood understood that in order to succeed in this endeavor, they needed to appeal to different strata of the American population in different ways; that whereas some people could be influenced by messages delivered from a religious perspective, others would be more responsive to messages delivered by educators, or bankers, or political figures, or journalists, etc. Thus, Akram's blueprint for the advancement of the Islamic movement stressed the need to form a coalition of groups coming from the worlds of education; religious proselytization; political activism; audio and video production; print media; banking and finance; the physical sciences; the social sciences; professional and business networking; cultural affairs; the publishing and distribution of books; children and teenagers; women's rights; vocational concerns; and jurisprudence.

By promoting the Islamic movement on such a wide variety of fronts, the Brotherhood and its allies could multiply exponentially their influence. Toward that end, the Akram/Brotherhood "Explanatory Memorandum" named the following 29 groups as the organizations they believed could collaborate effectively to destroy America from within – "if they all march according to one plan." This is that plan:

In the name of God, the Beneficent, the Merciful Thanks be to God, Lord of the Two Worlds, Prayers and peace be upon the master of the Messengers.

An Explanatory Memorandum
On the General Strategic Goal for the Group In North America
5/22/1991

Contents:
1- An introduction in explanation

35

2- The Concept of Settlement
3- The Process of Settlement
4- Comprehensive Settlement Organizations

The beloved brother/The General Masul, may God keep him.

The beloved brother/Secretary of the Shura Council, may God keep him.

The beloved brothers/Members of the Shura Council, may God keep them.

God's peace, mercy and blessings be upon you.... To proceed.

I ask Almighty God that you, your families and those whom you love around you are in the best of conditions, pleasing to God, glorified His name be.

I send this letter of mine to you hoping that it would seize your attention and receive your good care as you are the people of responsibility and those to whom trust is given. Between your hands is an "Explanatory Memorandum" which I put effort in writing down so that it is not locked in the chest and the mind, and so that I can share with you a portion of the responsibility in leading the Group in this country.

What might have encouraged me to submit the memorandum in this time in particular is my feeling of a "glimpse of hope" and the beginning of good tidings which bring the good news that we have embarked on a new stage of Islamic activism stages in this continent. The papers which are between your hands are not abundant extravagance, imaginations or hallucinations which passed in the mind of one of your brothers, but they are rather hopes, ambitions and challenges that I hope that you share some or most of which with me.

I do not claim their infallibility or absolute correctness, but they are an attempt which requires study, outlook, detailing and rooting from you.

My request to my brothers is to read the memorandum and to write what they wanted of comments and corrections, keeping in mind that what is between your hands is not strange or a new submission without a root, but rather an attempt to interpret and explain some of what came in the long-term plan which we approved and adopted in our council and our conference in the year (1987).

So, my honorable brother, do not rush to throw these papers away due to your many occupations and worries. All what I'm asking of you is to read them and to comment on them hoping that we might continue together the project of our plan and our Islamic work in this part of the world. Should you do that, I would be thankful and grateful to you.

I also ask my honorable brother, the Secretary of the Council, to add the subject of the memorandum on the Council agenda in its coming meeting.

God, the Beneficent, the Merciful Thanks be to God, Lord of the Two Worlds And Blessed are the Pious.

Subject: A project for an explanatory memorandum for the General Strategic goal for the Group in North America mentioned in the long-term plan

One: The Memorandum is derived from:

1- The general strategic goal of the Group in America which was approved by the Shura Council and the Organizational Conference for the year [1987] is "Enablement of Islam in North America, meaning:

establishing an effective and a stable Islamic Movement led by the Muslim Brotherhood which adopts Muslims' causes domestically and globally, and which works to expand the observant Muslim base, aims at unifying and directing Muslims' efforts, presents Islam as a civilization alternative, and supports the global Islamic State wherever it is."

2- The priority that is approved by the Shura Council for the work of the Group in its current and former session which is "Settlement".

3- The positive development with the brothers in the Islamic Circle in an attempt to reach a unity of merger.

4- The constant need for thinking and future planning, an attempt to read it and working to "shape" the present to comply and suit the needs and challenges of the future.

5- The paper of his eminence, the General Masul, may God keep him, which he recently sent to the members of the Council.

Two: An Introduction to the Explanatory Memorandum:

In order to begin with the explanation, we must "summon" the following question and place it in front of our eyes as its relationship is important and necessary with the strategic goal and the explanation project we are embarking on. The question we are facing is: "How do you like to see the Islam Movement in North America in ten years?", or "taking along" the following sentence when planning and working, "Islamic Work in North America in the year (2000): A Strategic Vision".

Also, we must summon and take along "elements" of the general strategic goal of the Group in North America and I will intentionally repeat them in numbers. They are:

1. Establishing an effective and stable Islamic Movement led by the Muslim Brotherhood.

2. Adopting Muslims' causes domestically and globally.

3. Expanding the observant Muslim base.

4. Unifying and directing Muslims' efforts.

5. Presenting Islam as a civilization alternative

6. Supporting the establishment of the global Islamic State wherever it is.

It must be stressed that it has become clear and emphatically known that all is in agreement that we must "settle" or "enable" Islam and its Movement in this part of the world. Therefore, a joint understanding of the meaning of settlement or enablement must be adopted, through which and on whose basis we explain the general strategic goal with its six elements for the Group in North America.

Three: The Concept of Settlement:

This term was mentioned in the Group's "dictionary" and documents with various meanings in spite of the fact that everyone meant one thing with it. We believe that the understanding of the essence is the same and we will attempt here to give the word and its "meanings" a practical explanation with a practical Movement tone, and not a philosophical linguistic explanation, while stressing that this explanation of ours is not complete until our explanation of "the process" of settlement itself is understood which is mentioned in the following paragraph. We briefly say the following:

Settlement: "That Islam and its Movement become a part of the homeland it lives in". Establishment: "That Islam turns into firmly-rooted organizations on whose bases civilization, structure and testimony are built". Stability: "That Islam is stable in the land on which its people move". Enablement: "That Islam is enabled within the souls, minds and the lives of the people of the country in which it moves". Rooting: "That Islam is resident and not a passing thing, or rooted "entrenched" in the soil of the spot where it moves and not a strange plant to it."

Four : The Process of Settlement:

In order for Islam and its Movement to become "a part of the homeland" in which it lives, "stable" in its land, "rooted" in the spirits and minds of its people, "enabled" in the live of its society and has firmly-established "organizations" on which the Islamic structure is built and with which the testimony of civilization is achieved, the Movement must plan and struggle to obtain "the keys" and the tools of this process in carry out this grand mission as a "Civilization Jihadist" responsibility which lies on the shoulders of Muslims and - on top of them - the Muslim Brotherhood in this country. Among these keys and tools are the following:

1- Adopting the concept of settlement and understanding its practical meanings:

The Explanatory Memorandum focused on the Movement and the realistic dimension of the process of settlement and its practical meanings without paying attention to the difference in understanding between the resident and the non-resident, or who is the settled and the non-settled and we believe that what was mentioned in the long-term plan in that regards suffices.

2- Making a fundamental shift in our thinking and mentality in order to suit the challenges of the settlement mission.

What is meant with the shift - which is a positive expression - is responding to the grand challenges of the settlement issues. We believe that any transforming response begins with the method of thinking and its center, the brain, first. In order to clarify what is meant with the shift as a key to qualify us to enter the field of settlement, we say very briefly that the following must be accomplished:

A shift from the partial thinking mentality to the comprehensive thinking mentality.

A shift from the "amputated" partial thinking mentality to the "continuous" comprehensive mentality.

A shift from the mentality of caution and reservation to the mentality of risk and controlled liberation.

A shift from the mentality of the elite Movement to the mentality of the popular Movement.

A shift from the mentality of preaching and guidance to the mentality of building and testimony.

A shift from the single opinion mentality to the multiple opinion mentality.

A shift from the collision mentality to the absorption mentality.

A shift from the individual mentality to the team mentality.

A shift from the anticipation mentality to the initiative mentality.

41

A shift from the hesitation mentality to the decisiveness mentality.

A shift from the principles mentality to the programs mentality.

A shift from the abstract ideas mentality the true organizations mentality [This is the core point and the essence of the memorandum].

3- Understanding the historical stages in which the Islamic Ikhwani activism went through in this country:

The writer of the memorandum believes that understanding and comprehending the historical stages of the Islamic activism which was led and being led by the Muslim Brotherhood in this continent is a very important key in working towards settlement, through which the Group observes its march, the direction of its movement and the curves and turns of its road. We will suffice here with mentioning the title for each of these stages [The title expresses the prevalent characteristic of the stage] [Details maybe mentioned in another future study]. Most likely, the stages are:

A- The stage of searching for self and determining the identity.

B- The stage of inner build-up and tightening the organization.

C- The stage of mosques and the Islamic centers.

D- The stage of building the Islamic organizations - the first phase.

E- The stage of building the Islamic schools - the first phase.

F- The stage of thinking about the overt Islamic Movement - the first phase.

G- The stage of openness to the other Islamic movements and attempting to reach a formula for dealing with them - the first phase.

H- The stage of reviving and establishing the Islamic organizations - the second phase.

We believe that the Group is embarking on this stage in its second phase as it has to open the door and enter as it did the first time.

4-Understanding the role of the Muslim Brother in North America:

The process of settlement is a "Civilization-Jihadist Process" with all the word means. The Ikhwan must understand that their work in America is a kind of grand Jihad in eliminating and destroying the Western civilization from within and "sabotaging" its miserable house by their hands and the hands of the believers so that it is eliminated and God's religion is made victorious over all other religions. Without this level of understanding, we are not up to this challenge and have not prepared ourselves for Jihad yet. It is a Muslim's destiny to perform Jihad and work wherever he is and wherever he lands until the final hour comes, and there is no escape from that destiny except for those who chose to slack. But, would the slackers and the Mujahedeen be equal.

5-Understanding that we cannot perform the settlement mission by ourselves or away from people:

A mission as significant and as huge as the settlement mission needs magnificent and exhausting efforts. With their capabilities, human, financial and scientific resources, the Ikhwan will not be able to carry out this mission alone or away from people and he who believes that is wrong, and God knows best. As for the role of the Ikhwan, it is the initiative, pioneering, leadership, raising the banner and pushing people in that direction. They are then to work to employ, direct and unify Muslims' efforts and powers for this process. In order to do that, we must possess a mastery of the art of "coalitions", the art of "absorption" and the principles of "cooperation".

6-The necessity of achieving a union and balanced gradual merger between private work and public work:

We believe that what was written about this subject is many and is enough. But, it needs a time and a practical frame so that what is needed is achieved in a gradual and a balanced way that is compatible with the process of settlement.

7-The conviction that the success of the settlement of Islam and its Movement in this country is a success to the global Islamic Movement and a true support for the sought-after state, God willing:

There is a conviction - with which this memorandum disagrees - that our focus in attempting to settle Islam in this country will lead to negligence in our duty towards the global Islamic Movement in supporting its project to establish the state. We believe that the reply is in two segments: One - The success of the Movement in America in establishing an observant Islamic base with power and effectiveness will be the best support and aid to the global Movement project. And the second - is the global Movement has not succeeded yet in "distributing roles" to its branches, stating what is the needed from them as one of the participants or contributors to the project to establish the global Islamic state. The day this happens, the children of the American Ikhwani branch will have far-reaching impact and positions that make the ancestors proud.

8-Absorbing Muslims and winning them with all of their factions and colors in America and Canada for the settlement project, and making it their cause, future and the basis of their Islamic life in this part of the world:

This issue requires from us to learn "the art of dealing with the others", as people are different and people in many colors. We need to adopt the principle which says, "Take from people... the best they have", their best specializations, experiences, arts, energies and abilities. By people here we mean those within or without the ranks of individuals and organizations. The policy of "taking" should be with what achieves the strategic goal and the settlement process. But the big challenge in front of us is: how to connect them all in "the orbit" of our plan and "the circle" of our Movement in order to achieve "the core" of our interest. To me, there is no choice for us other than alliance and mutual understanding of those who desire from our religion and those who agree from our belief in work. And the U.S. Islamic arena is full of those waiting...., the pioneers.

What matters is bringing people to the level of comprehension of the challenge that is facing us as Muslims in this country, conviction of our settlement project, and understanding the benefit of agreement, cooperation and alliance. At that time, if we ask for money, a lot of it would come, and if we ask for men, they would come in lines. What matters is that our plan is "the criterion and the balance" in our relationship with others.

Here, two points must be noted; the first one: we need to comprehend and understand the balance of the Islamic powers in the U.S. arena [and this might be the subject of a future study]. The second point: what we reached with the brothers in "ICNA" is considered a step in the right direction, the beginning of good and the first drop that requires growing and guidance.

9-Re-examining our organizational and administrative bodies, the type of leadership and the method of selecting it with what suits the challenges of the settlement mission:

The memorandum will be silent about details regarding this item even though it is logical and there is a lot to be said about it,

10-Growing and developing our resources and capabilities, our financial and human resources with what suits the magnitude of the grand mission:

If we examined the human and the financial resources the Ikhwan alone own in this country, we and others would feel proud and glorious. And if we add to them the resources of our friends and allies, those who circle in our orbit and those waiting on our banner, we would realize that we are able to open the door to settlement and walk through it seeking to make Almighty God's word the highest.

11-Utilizing the scientific method in planning, thinking and preparation of studies needed for the process of settlement:

Yes, we need this method, and we need many studies which aid in this civilization Jihadist operation. We will mention some of them briefly:

The history of the Islamic presence in America. The history of the Islamic Ikhwani presence in America. Islamic movements, organizations and organizations: analysis and criticism. The phenomenon of the Islamic centers and schools: challenges, needs and statistics.Islamic minorities, Muslim and Arab communities.

The U.S. society: make-up and politics. The U.S. society's view of Islam and Muslims... And many other studies which we can direct our brothers and allies to prepare, either through their academic studies or through their educational centers or organizational tasking. What is important is that we start.

12-Agreeing on a flexible, balanced and a clear "mechanism" to implement the process of settlement within a specific, gradual and balanced "time frame" that is in-line with the demands and challenges of the process of settlement.

13-Understanding the U.S. society from its different aspects an understanding that "qualifies" us to perform the mission of settling our Dawa' in its country "and growing it" on its land.

14-Adopting a written "jurisprudence" that includes legal and movement bases, principles, policies and interpretations which are suitable for the needs and challenges of the process of settlement.

15-Agreeing on "criteria" and balances to be a sort of "antennas" or "the watch tower" in order to make sure that all of our priorities, plans, programs, bodies, leadership, monies and activities march towards the process of the settlement.

16-Adopting a practical, flexible formula through which our central work complements our domestic work.
[Items 12 through 16 will be detailed later].

17-Understanding the role and the nature of work of "The Islamic Center" in every city with what achieves the goal of the process of settlement:

The center we seek is the one which constitutes the "axis" of our Movement, the "perimeter" of the circle of our work, our "balance center", the "base" for our rise and our "Dar al-Arqam" to educate us, prepare us and supply our battalions in addition to being the "niche" of our prayers.

This is in order for the Islamic center to turn - in action not in words - into a seed "for a small Islamic society" which is a reflection and a mirror to our central organizations. The center ought to turn into a "beehive" which produces sweet honey. Thus, the Islamic center would turn into a place for study, family, battalion, course, seminar, visit, sport, school, social club, women gathering, kindergarten for male and female youngsters, the office of the domestic political resolution, and the center for distributing our newspapers, magazines, books and our audio and visual tapes.

In brief we say: we would like for the Islamic center to become "The House of Dawa'" and "the general center" in deeds first before name. As much as we own and direct these centers at the continent level, we can say we are marching successfully towards the settlement of Dawa' in this country.

Meaning that the "center's" role should be the same as the "mosque's" role during the time of God's prophet, God's prayers and peace be upon him, when he marched to "settle" the Dawa' in its first generation in Madina. from the mosque, he drew the Islamic life and provided to the world the most magnificent and fabulous civilization humanity knew.

This mandates that, eventually, the region, the branch and the Usra turn into "operations rooms" for planning, direction, monitoring and leadership for the Islamic center in order to be a role model to be followed.

18-Adopting a system that is based on "selecting" workers, "role distribution" and "assigning" positions and responsibilities is based on specialization, desire and need with what achieves the process of settlement and contributes to its success.

19-Turning the principle of dedication for the Masuls of main positions within the Group into a rule, a basis and a policy in work. Without it, the process of settlement might be stalled [Talking about this point requires more details and discussion].

20-Understanding the importance of the "Organizational" shift in our Movement work, and doing Jihad in order to achieve it in the real world with what serves the process of settlement and expedites its results, God Almighty's willing:

The reason this paragraph was delayed is to stress its utmost importance as it constitutes the heart and the core of this memorandum. It also constitutes the practical aspect and the true measure of our success or failure in our march towards settlement. The talk about the organizations and the "organizational" mentality or phenomenon does not require much details. It suffices to say that the first pioneer of this phenomenon was our prophet Mohamed, God's peace, mercy and blessings be upon him, as he placed the foundation for the first civilized organization which is the mosque, which truly became "the comprehensive organization". And this was done by the pioneer of the contemporary Islamic Dawa', Imam martyr Hasan al-Banna, may God have mercy on him, when he and his brothers felt the need to "re-establish" Islam and its movement anew, leading him to establish organizations with all their kinds: economic, social, media, scouting, professional and even the military ones. We must say that we are in a country which understands no language other than the language of the organizations, and one which does not respect or give weight to any group without effective, functional and strong organizations.

It is good fortune that there are brothers among us who have this "trend", mentality or inclination to build the organizations who have beat us by action and words which leads us to dare say honestly what Sadat in Egypt once said, "We want to build a country of organizations" - a word of right he meant wrong with. I say to my brothers, let us raise the banner of truth to establish right "We want to establish Group organizations", as without it we will not able to put our feet on the true path.

And in order for the process of settlement to be completed, we must plan and work from now to equip and prepare ourselves, our brothers, our apparatuses, our sections and our committees in order to turn into comprehensive organizations in a gradual and balanced way that is suitable with the need and the reality. What encourages us to do that - in addition to the aforementioned -is that we possess "seeds" for each organization from the organization we call for.

All we need is to tweak them, coordinate their work, collect their elements and merge their efforts with others and then connect them with the comprehensive plan we seek.

For instance, We have a seed for a "comprehensive media and art" organization: we own a print + advanced typesetting machine + audio and visual center + art production office + magazines in Arabic and English [The Horizons, The Hope, The Politicians, Ha Falastine, Press Clips, al-Zaytouna, Palestine Monitor, Social Sciences Magazines...] + art band + photographers + producers + programs anchors + journalists + in addition to other media and art experiences". Another example:

We have a seed for a "comprehensive Dawa' educational" organization: We have the Daw'a section in ISNA + Dr. Jamal Badawi Foundation + the center run by brother Hamed al-Ghazali + the Dawa' center the Dawa' Committee and brother Shaker al-Sayyed are seeking to establish now + in addition to other Daw'a efforts here and there...". And this applies to all the organizations we call on establishing.

The big challenge that is ahead of us is how to turn these seeds or "scattered" elements into comprehensive, stable, "settled" organizations that are connected with our Movement and which fly in our orbit and take orders from our guidance. This does not prevent - but calls for - each central organization to have its local branches but its connection with the Islamic center in the city is a must.

What is needed is to seek to prepare the atmosphere and the means to achieve "the merger" so that the sections, the committees, the regions, the branches and the Usras are eventually the heart and the core of these organizations. Or, for the shift and the change to occur as follows:

1- The Movement Department + The Secretariat Department
2- Education Department + Dawa'a Com.
3- Sisters Department
4- The Financial Department + Investment Committee + The Endowment
5- Youth Department + Youths Organizations Department
6- The Social Committee + Matrimony Committee + Mercy Foundation
7- The Security Committee
8- The Political Depart. + Palestine Com.
9- The Group's Court + The Legal Com.
10-Domestic Work Department
11- Our magazines + the print + our art band
12- The Studies Association + The Publication House + Dar al-Kitab
13- Scientific and Medial societies
14- The Organizational Conference
15- The Shura Council + Planning Com.

16- The Executive Office
17- The General Masul
18- The regions, branches & Usras

The Organizational & Administrative Organization

The General Center
Dawa' and Educational Organization
The Women's Organization
The Economic Organization
Youth Organizations
The Social Organization
The Security Organization
The Political Organization
The Judicial Organization
Its work is to be distributed to the rest of the organizations
The Media and Art Organization
The Intellectual & Cultural Organization
Scientific, Educational & Professional Organization
The Islamic-American Founding Conference
The Shura Council for the Islamic-American Movement
The Executive Office of the Islamic-American Movement
Chairman of the Islamic Movement and its official Spokesman
Field leaders of organizations & Islamic centers

Five: Comprehensive Settlement Organization:

We would then seek and struggle in order to make each one of these above-mentioned organizations a "comprehensive organization" throughout the days and the years, and as long as we are destined to be in this country. What is important is that we put the foundation and we will be followed by peoples and generations that would finish the march and the road but with a clearly-defined guidance.

And, in order for us to clarify what we mean with the comprehensive, specialized organization, we mention here the characteristics and traits of each organization of the "promising" organizations.

1-From the Dawa' and educational aspect [The Dawa* and Educational Organization]: to include:

The Organization to spread the Dawa' (Central and local branches).
An institute to graduate Callers and Educators.
Scholars, Callers, Educators, Preachers and Program Anchors.
Art and communication technology, Conveyance and Dawa'.
A television station.
A specialized Dawa' magazine.
A radio station.
The Higher Islamic Council for Callers and Educators.
The Higher Council for Mosques and Islamic Centers.
Friendship Societies with the other religions... and things like that.

2-Politically [The Political Organization]: to include:

A central political party.
Local political offices.
Political symbols.
Relationships and alliances.
The American Organization for Islamic Political Action
Advanced Information Centers....and things like that.

3-Media [The Media and Art Organization]: to include:

A daily newspaper,
Weekly, monthly and seasonal magazines.
Radio stations.
Television programs.
Audio and visual centers.

A magazine for the Muslim child.
A magazine for the Muslim woman.
A print and typesetting machines.
A production office.
A photography and recording studio
Art bands for acting, chanting and theater.
A marketing and art production office... and things like that.

4-Economically [The Economic Organization!: to include:

An Islamic Central bank.
Islamic endowments.
Investment projects.
An organization for interest-free loans.... and things like that.

5-Scientifically and Professionally [The Scientific. Educational and Professional Organization]: to include:

Scientific research centers.
Technical organizations and vocational training.
An Islamic university.
Islamic schools.
A council for education and scientific research.
Centers to train teachers.
Scientific societies in schools.
An office for academic guidance.
A body for authorship and Islamic curricula.... and things like that.

6-Culturally and Intellectually [The Cultural and Intellectual Organization]: to include:

A center for studies and research.

Cultural and intellectual foundations such as [The Social Scientists Society - Scientists and Engineers Society....].
An organization for Islamic thought and culture.
A publication, translation and distribution house for Islamic books.
An office for archiving, history and authentication
The project to translate the Noble Quran, the Noble Sayings....and things like that.

7-Socially [The Social-Charitable Organization]: to include:

Social clubs for the youths and the community's sons and daughters.
Local societies for social welfare and the services are tied to the Islamic centers.
The Islamic Organization to Combat the Social Ills of the U.S. Society.
Islamic houses project.
Matrimony and family cases office....and things like that.

8-Youths [The Youth Organization]: to include:

Central and local youths foundations.
Sports teams and clubs
Scouting teams....and things like that.

9-Women [The Women Organization]: to include:

Central and local women societies.
Organizations of training, vocational and housekeeping.
An organization to train female preachers.
Islamic kindergartens...and things like that.

10-Organizationally and Administratively [The Administrative and Organizational Organization]: to include:

An institute for training, growth, development and planning
Prominent experts in this field
Work systems, bylaws and charters fit for running the most complicated bodies and organizations
A periodic magazine in Islamic development and administration.
Owning camps and halls for the various activities.
A data, polling and census bank.
An advanced communication network.
An advanced archive for our heritage and production....and things like that.

11-Security [The Security Organization]: to include:

Clubs for training and learning self-defense techniques.
A center which is concerned with the security issues [Technical, intellectual, technological and human]....and things like that.

12-Legally [The Legal Organization]: to include:

A Central Jurisprudence Council.
A Central Islamic Court.
Muslim Attorneys Society.
The Islamic Foundation for Defense of Muslims' Rights...and things like that. And success is by God.

Attachment

A list of our organizations and the organizations of our friends [Imagine if they all march according to one plan!!!]

AMSE--The Association of Muslim Scientists and Engineers
IMA----Islamic Medical Association
ITC-----Islamic Teaching Center
NAIT---North American Islamic Trust
FID-----Foundation for International Development
IHC----Islamic Housing Cooperative
ICD----Islamic Centers Division
ATP---American Trust Publications
AVC---Audio-Visual Center
IBS----Islamic Book Service
MBA----Muslim Businessmen Association
MYNA----Muslim Youth of North America
IFC ISNA----FIQH Committee
IPAC-ISNA----Political Awareness Committee
IED----Islamic Education Department
MAYA----Muslim Arab Youth Association
MISG----Malasian Islamic Study Group
IAP----Islamic Association for Palestine
UASR----United Association for Studies and Research
OLF----Occupied Land Fund
MIA----Mercy International Association
ICNA----Islamic Circle of North America
BMI----Baitul Mal Inc.
IIIT----International Institute for Islamic Thought
IC----Islamic Information Center
CAIR—Council on American-Islamic Relations

This is the Islamic plan for their 'Silent Jihad.' It's already well-advanced in our nation. And, too many are turning their backs and closing their eyes; and closing their ears not to see it, hear it, or understand it. Our national leaders are not only refusing to challenge this silent Jihad, they seem to be encouraging it and supporting it - even financially.

Chapter 3
Supporting the Muslim Brotherhood

Not too long ago, Obama strongly supported Morsi, of the Muslim Brotherhood, as the president of Egypt, refusing to offer support to Egypt when Morsi was overthrown. Following is an example of his support to the Muslim Brotherhood - the architect of that plan to destroy the United States from within. It involves a large sum of money offered to Morsi. This report by Kristin Tate at mrconservative.com. gives that information:

"Secretary of State John Kerry secretly gave $1.3 billion to Egypt, which is controlled by the Muslim Brotherhood." (This was before the Muslim Brotherhood's Morsi was ousted by the military.) The article continues:

"To give this "gift", Kerry had to waive restrictions put in place by Congress, which forbid giving US military aid unless the country meets certain basic democracy standards. The secretary of state is supposed to certify that the recipient country's government is "supporting the transition to civilian government, including holding free and fair elections, implementing policies to protect freedom of expression, association and religion, and due process of law." By law, the State Department may only give Egypt aid each year if the secretary of state certifies that Egypt is honoring its peace treaty with Israel.

This is clearly not happening in Egypt. The country is currently run by the Muslim Brotherhood, (at that time) a large and dangerous terrorist organization.

The substantial gift goes against what Kerry has said of Egypt in the recent past. On May 9th, he said, "We are not satisfied with the extent of Egypt's progress and are pressing for a more inclusive democratic process and strengthening of key democratic institutions." Why, then, are you giving them $1.3 billion of our precious dollars, Kerry?

He continued, "A strong U.S. security partnership with Egypt, underpinned by FMF (Foreign Military Financing), maintains a channel to Egyptian military leadership, who are key opinion makers in the country. A decision to waive restrictions on FMF to Egypt is necessary to uphold these interests as we encourage Egypt to continue its transition to democracy."

The State Department's notification of Kerry's secretive move was never released to the public… until now.

Former Secretary of State Hilary Clinton also waived the restriction, but was much more transparent about it. The decision was announced publicly and defended to the media.

The executive director of the Project on Middle East Democracy, Stephen McInerney, said it is "very alarming that no public statement was made by the secretary or the Department of State more broadly in conjunction with the waiving of these conditions."

What makes the aid decision worse was Egypt's sentencing American NGO workers, who were only there to help build and promote democracy in the country. End of article.

And, we have another more direct supporter of the Muslim Brother right by Hillary Clinton's side – at all times. It's her close advisor and confident, Huma Abedin. Who is this Huma that's so respected and supported by Hillary? Let's examine her background and inclinations more closely. This information is from this link:

http://www.discoverthenetworks.org/individualProfile.asp?indid=2 556

"Daughter of Saleha Mahmood Abedin, a pro-Sharia sociologist with ties to numerous Islamist organizations including the Muslim Brotherhood

Longtime assistant to Hillary Clinton

Wife of former congressman Anthony Weiner

Longtime former employee of the Institute of Muslim Minority Affairs, which shares the Muslim Brotherhood's goal of establishing Islamic supremacy and Sharia Law worldwide.

Huma Abedin was born in 1976 in Kalamazoo, Michigan. Her father, Syed Abedin (1928-1993), was an Indian-born scholar who in the early 1970s had been affiliated with the Muslim Students Association at Western Michigan University. Huma's mother, Saleha Mahmood Abedin, is a sociologist known for her strong advocacy of Sharia Law. A member of the Muslim Sisterhood (i.e., the Muslim Brotherhood's division for women), Saleha is also a board member of the International Islamic Council for Dawa and Relief. This pro-Hamas entity is part of the Union of Good, which the U.S.

government has formally designated as an international terrorist organization led by the Muslim Brotherhood luminary Yusuf al-Qaradawi.

When Huma was two, the Abedin family relocated from Michigan to Jeddah, Saudi Arabia. This move took place when Abdullah Omar Naseef, a major Muslim Brotherhood figure who served as vice president of Abdulaziz University (AU), recruited his former AU colleague, Syed Abedin, to work for the Institute of Muslim Minority Affairs (IMMA), a Saudi-based Islamic think tank that Naseef was preparing to launch.

A number of years later, Naseef would develop close ties to Osama bin Laden and the terrorist group al-Qaeda. Naseef also spent time (beginning in the early 1980s) as secretary-general of the Muslim World League, which, as journalist Andrew C. McCarthy points out, "has long been the Muslim Brotherhood's principal vehicle for the international propagation of Islamic supremacist ideology." IMMA's close ties to the Muslim World League are further evidenced by the fact that IMMA's in-house publication, the Journal of Muslim Minority Affairs (JMMA), has long listed its official address as 46 Goodge Street in London -- precisely the same address as that of the Muslim World League's London office. It is vital to note that IMMA's "Muslim Minority Affairs" agenda was, and remains to this day, a calculated foreign policy of the Saudi Ministry of Religious Affairs, designed, as Andrew C. McCarthy explains, "to grow an unassimilated, aggressive population of Islamic supremacists who will gradually but dramatically alter the character of the West."

At age 18, Huma Abedin returned to the U.S. to attend George Washington University. In 1996 she began working as an intern in the Bill Clinton White House, where she was assigned to then-First Lady Hillary Rodham Clinton. Abedin was eventually hired as an aide to Mrs. Clinton and has worked for her ever since, through Clinton's successful Senate runs (in 2000 and 2006) and her failed presidential bid in 2008. From 1997 until sometime before early 1999, Abedin, while still interning at the White House, was an executive board member of George Washington University's (GWU) Muslim Students Association (MSA), heading the organization's "Social Committee."

It is noteworthy that in 2001-02, soon after Abedin left that executive board, the chaplain and "spritual guide" of GWU's MSA was Anwar al-Awlaki, the al-Qaeda operative who ministered to some of the men who were among the 9/11 hijackers. Another chaplain at GWU's MSA (from at least October 1999 through April 2002) was Mohamed Omeish, who headed the International Islamic Relief Organization, which has been tied to the funding of al-Qaeda. Omeish's brother, Esam, headed the Muslim American Society, the Muslim Brotherhood's quasi-official branch in the United States. Both Omeish brothers were closely associated with Abdurahman Alamoudi, who would later be convicted and incarcerated on terrorism charges.

From 1996-2008, Abedin was employed by the Institute of Muslim Minority Affairs (IMMA) as the assistant editor of its aforementioned publication, the Journal of Muslim Minority Affairs(JMMA). At least the first seven of those years overlapped with the al Qaeda-affiliated Abdullah Omar Naseef's active presence at IMMA. Abedin's last six years at the Institute (2002-2008) were spent as a JMMA editorial board member; for one of those years, 2003, Naseef and Abedin served together on that board.

Throughout her years with IMMA, Abedin remained a close aide to Hillary Clinton. During Mrs. Clinton's 2008 presidential primary campaign, a New York Observer profile of Abedin described her as "a trusted advisor to Mrs. Clinton, especially on issues pertaining to the Middle East, according to a number of Clinton associates." "At meetings on the region," continued the profile, "... Ms. Abedin's perspective is always sought out." When Mrs. Clinton was appointed as President Barack Obama's Secretary of State in 2009, Abedin became her deputy chief of staff. At approximately that same point in time, Abedin's name was removed from the Journal of Muslim Minority Affairs' masthead.

Apart from their working relationship, Abedin and Mrs. Clinton have also developed a close personal bond over their years together, as reflected in Clinton's 2010 assertion that: "I have one daughter. But if I had a second daughter, it would [be] Huma." In 2011, Secretary Clinton paid a friendly visit to Abedin's mother, Saleha, in Saudi Arabia. On that occasion, Mrs. Clinton publicly described her aide's position as "very important and sensitive."

On July 10, 2010, Huma Abedin, a practicing Muslim, married then-congressman Anthony Weiner in a ceremony officiated by former president Bill Clinton. A number of analysts have noted that it is extremely rare for Islamic women—particularly those whose families have ties to the Muslim Brotherhood—to marry non-Muslims like Weiner, who is Jewish. Indeed, Dr. Anwar Shoeb, the highest-ranking faculty authority at the prestigious College of Sharia and Islamic Studies in Kuwait, formally declared that Abedin's marriage to Weiner was "null and void" under the dictates of Sharia Law, which explicitly forbids matrimony between a Muslim woman and an "infidel"; in fact, Shoeb classified the Abedin-Weiner union as a form of "adultery."

Abedin went on maternity leave after giving birth to a baby boy in early December 2011. When she returned to work in June 2012, the State Department granted her an arrangement that allowed her to earn outside income as a private consultant, even as she remained a top advisor in the Department. This arrangement was made possible when Mrs. Clinton personally signed off on documents—dated March 23,

2012—that changed Abedin's title from "deputy chief off staff" to "special government employee." Abedin's outside clients included the U.S. State Department, Hillary Clinton, the Clinton Foundation, and Teneo (a New York-based global advisory firm co-founded by Doug Band, a former counselor for Bill Clinton.

Abedin did not disclose on her financial report either the special employment arrangement or the $135,000 she earned from it, in violation of a law mandating that public officials reveal significant sources of income. In fact, her title change did not become public knowledge until May 2013. Good-government groups warned of the potential conflict-of-interest inherent in an arrangement where a government employee maintains private clients.

Documents obtained by Judicial Watch in a Freedom Of Information Act (FOIA) lawsuit showed that both before and after Mrs. Clinton signed off on the special employment deal for Abedin in March 2012, Abedin repeatedly—for months on end—dodged State Department requests that she disclose financial and employment information about her husband, Anthony Weiner, who had left Congress amid personal scandal in June 2011.

In June 2012, five Republican lawmakers (most prominently, Michele Bachmann) sent letters to the inspectors general at the Departments of Homeland Security, Justice, and State, asking that they investigate whether the Muslim Brotherhood was gaining undue influence over U.S. government officials. One letter, noting that Huma Abedin's position with Hillary Clinton "affords her routine access to the secretary [of state] and to policymaking," expressed concern over the fact that Abedin "has three family members—her late father, mother and her brother—connected to Muslim Brotherhood operatives and/or organizations." Some other prominent Republicans such as John McCain and John Boehner disavowed the concerns articulated in the letters.

On February 1, 2013—Hillary Clinton's final day as Secretary of State—Abedin resigned her post as Mrs. Clinton's deputy chief of staff. Yet she would continue to serve as a close aide to Clinton. On March 1, 2013, Abedin was tapped to run Clinton's post-State Department transition team, comprised of a six-person "transition office" located in Washington.

In early March 2015, it was reported that throughout her entire four-year tenure as Secretary of State (SOS), Hillary Clinton had never acquired or used a government email account, and instead had transmitted -- in violation of government regulations -- all of her official government correspondences via a personal email account that was housed on a private server. In addition, Abedin and Mrs. Clinton's chief of staff, Cheryl Mills, also had email addresses on the secret server while employed at the State Department.

After Hillary Clinton announced in the spring of 2015 that she was running for president (2016), Abedin was named vice chair of the Clinton campaign.

Huma Abedin's brother, Hassan Abedin, has ties to the Muslim Brotherhood and is currently an associate editor with the JMMA. Hassan was once a fellow at the Oxford Center for Islamic Studies, at a time when the Center's board included such Brotherhood-affiliated figures as Yusuf al-Qaradawi and Abdullah Omar Naseef.

Huma's sister, Heba Abedin (formerly known as "Heba A. Khaled"), is an assistant editor with JMMA, where she served alongside Huma prior to the latter's departure."

Not only does Hillary Clinton have close ties to Muslim Brotherhood associates and contacts, which puts our nation at risk from that deadly Muslim Brotherhood threat, she also has a history of close ties to others presenting a different danger. One is her long-ago close association and support to Saul Alinsky. Let's examine that close association to understand that threat.

Chapter 4
Saul Alinsky and Hillary Clinton

Hillary Clinton's association with Saul Alinsky began early in her life, while she was in school. This information from Freebeacon.com introduces the beginning of that relationship. The article was submitted by Alana Goodman on 21 September, 2014:

"Previously unpublished correspondence between Hillary Clinton and the late left-wing organizer Saul Alinsky reveals new details about her relationship with the controversial Chicago activist and shed light on her early ideological development.

Clinton met with Alinsky several times in 1968 while writing a Wellesley college thesis about his theory of community organizing. Clinton's relationship with Alinsky, and her support for his philosophy, continued for several years after she entered Yale law school in 1969, two letters obtained by the Washington Free Beacon show.

The letters obtained by the Free Beacon are part of the archives for the Industrial Areas Foundation, a training center for community organizers founded by Alinsky, which are housed at the University of Texas at Austin. The letters also suggest that Alinsky, who died in 1972, had a deeper influence on Clinton's early political views than previously known.

A 23-year-old Hillary Clinton was living in Berkeley, California, in the summer of 1971. She was interning at the left-wing law firm Treuhaft, Walker and Burnstein, known for its radical politics and a client roster that included Black Panthers and other militants.

On July 8, 1971, Clinton reached out to Alinsky, then 62, in a letter sent via airmail, paid for with stamps featuring Franklin Delano Roosevelt, and marked "Personal."

"Dear Saul," she began. "When is that new book [Rules for Radicals] coming out—or has it come and I somehow missed the fulfillment of Revelation?"

"I have just had my one-thousandth conversation about Reveille [for Radicals] and need some new material to throw at people," she added, a reference to Alinsky's 1946 book on his theories of community organizing.

Clinton devoted just one paragraph in her memoir Living History to Alinsky, writing that she rejected a job offer from him in 1969 in favor of going to law school. She wrote that she wanted to follow a more conventional path.

However, in the 1971 letter, Clinton assured Alinsky that she had "survived law school, slightly bruised, with my belief in and zest for organizing intact."

"The more I've seen of places like Yale Law School and the people who haunt them, the more convinced I am that we have the serious business and joy of much work ahead—if the commitment to a free and open society is ever going to mean more than eloquence and frustration," wrote Clinton.

According to the letter, Clinton and Alinsky had kept in touch since she entered Yale. The 62-year-old radical had reached out to give her advice on campus activism.

"If I never thanked you for the encouraging words of last spring in the midst of the Yale-Cambodia madness, I do so now," wrote Clinton, who had moderated a campus election to join an anti-war student strike.

She added that she missed their regular conversations, and asked if Alinsky would be able to meet her the next time he was in California.

"I am living in Berkeley and working in Oakland for the summer and would love to see you," Clinton wrote. "Let me know if there is any chance of our getting together."

Clinton's letter reached Alinsky's office while he was on an extended trip to Southeast Asia, where he was helping train community organizers in the Philippines.

But a response letter from Alinsky's secretary suggests that the radical organizer had a deep fondness for Clinton as well.

"Since I know [Alinsky's] feelings about you I took the liberty of opening your letter because I didn't want something urgent to wait for two weeks," Alinsky's long-time secretary, Georgia Harper, wrote to Clinton in a July 13, 1971 letter. "And I'm glad I did."

Harper told Clinton that Alinksy's book Rules for Radicals had been released. She enclosed several reviews of the book.

"Mr. Alinsky will be in San Francisco, staying at the Hilton Inn at the airport on Monday and Tuesday, July 26 and 27," Harper added. "I know he would like to have you call him so that if there is a chance in his schedule maybe you can get together."

71

It is unclear whether the meeting occurred.

A self-proclaimed radical, Alinsky advocated guerilla tactics and civil disobedience to correct what he saw as an institutionalized power gap in poor communities. His philosophy divided the world into "haves"—middle class and wealthy people —and "have nots"—the poor. He took an ends-justify-the-means approach to power and wealth redistribution, and developed the theoretical basis of "community organizing."

"The Prince was written by Machiavelli for the Haves on how to hold power," wrote Alinsky in his 1971 book. "Rules for Radicals is written for the Have-Nots on how to take it away."

Clinton's connection to Alinsky has been the subject of speculation for decades. It became controversial when Wellsley College, by request of the Clinton White House, sealed her 1968 thesis from the public for years. Conservative lawyer Barbara Olson said Clinton had asked for the thesis to be sealed because it showed "the extent to which she internalized and assimilated the beliefs and methods of Saul Alinsky." Clinton opponent turned Clinton defender David Brock referred to her as "Alinsky's daughter" in 1996's The Seduction of Hillary Rodham.

The paper was opened to the public in 2001. While the thesis is largely sympathetic to Alinsky, it is also critical of some of his tactics.

Clinton described the organizer as "a man of exceptional charm," but also objected to some of the conflicts he provoked as "unrealistic," noting that his model could be difficult for others to replicate.

"Many of the Alinsky-inspired poverty warriors could not (discounting political reasons) move beyond the cathartic first step of organizing groups 'to oppose, complain, demonstrate, and boycott' to developing and running a program," she wrote.

The letters obtained by the Free Beacon suggest that Clinton experimented more with radical politics during her law school years than she has publicly acknowledged.

In Living History, she describes her views during that time as far more pragmatic than leftwing.

She "agreed with some of Alinsky's ideas," Clinton wrote in her first memoir, but the two had a "fundamental disagreement" over his anti-establishment tactics.

She described how this disagreement led to her parting ways with Alinsky in the summer before law school in 1969.

"He offered me the chance to work with him when I graduated from college, and he was disappointed that I decided instead to go to law school," she wrote.

"Alinsky said I would be wasting my time, but my decision was an expression of my belief that the system could be changed from within."

A request for comment from the Clinton team was not returned.

The author of this article, Alana Goodman, is a staff writer for the Washington Free Beacon. Prior to joining the Beacon, she was assistant online editor at Commentary. She has written for the Weekly Standard, the New York Post and the Washington Examiner. End of article.

This is a full typed copy of the original version of Clinton's letter with addresses included:

July 8, 1971
Berkeley

Dear Saul,

When is that new book coming out - or has it come and I somehow missed the fulfillment of Revelation? I have just had my one-thousandth conversation about <u>Reveille</u> and need some new material to throw at people. You are being rediscovered again as the New Left-type politicos are finally beginning to think seriously about the hard work and mechanics of organizing.

I seem to have survived law school, slightly bruised, with my belief in and zest for organizing intact. If I never thanked you for the encouraging words of last spring in the midst of the Yale-Cambodia madness, I do so now. The more I've seen of places like Yale Law School and the people who haunt them, the more convinced I am that we have the serious business and joy of much work ahead,-- if the commitment to a free and open society is ever going to seem more than eloquence and frustration.

I miss our biennial conversations. Do you ever make it out to California? I am living in Berkeley and working in Oakland for the summer and would love to see you. Let me know if there is any chance of our getting together -- 2667 Derby #2, Berkeley 415-841-5330.

There were rumors of your going to SE Asia to recruit organizers. Is the lack of imagination among my peers really so rampant as that suggests or did you get yourself a CIA-sponsored junket to exotica?

I hope you are still well and fighting. Give my regards to Mrs. Harper. Hopefully we can have a good argument sometime in the near future.

Until then --
Hillary (Signed)

Envelope:
(From)
Hillary Rodham
2667 Derby #2
Berkeley, CA 94705

(To)
MR. SAUL ALINSKY
c/o The Industrial Areas Foundation
8 South Michigan Ave.
Chicago, Illinois

This is another article, from Wikipedia, the free encyclopedia, that gives even more information about Hillary's fascination with the work of Saul Alinsky:

"In 1969, Hillary Rodham wrote a 92-page senior thesis for Wellesley College titled "There Is Only the Fight . . . An Analysis of the Alinsky Model". The subject was famed radical community organizer Saul Alinsky.

Contents

1 Thesis
2 White House and Wellesley limiting of access
3 Thesis unveiled
4 References

Thesis:

The thesis offered a critique of Alinsky's methods as largely ineffective, all the while describing Alinsky's personality as appealing. The thesis sought to fit Alinsky into a line of American social activists, including Eugene V. Debs, Martin Luther King, Jr., and Walt Whitman. Written in formal academic language, the thesis concluded that "[Alinsky's] power/conflict model is rendered inapplicable by existing social conflicts" and that Alinsky's model had not expanded nationally due to "the anachronistic nature of small autonomous conflict."

In the acknowledgements and end notes of the thesis, Rodham thanked Alinsky for two interviews and a job offer. She declined the latter, saying that "after spending a year trying to make sense out of [Alinsky's] inconsistency, I need three years of legal rigor." Rodham, an honors student at Wellesley, received an A grade on the thesis.

White House and Wellesley limiting of access:

The work was unnoticed until Hillary Rodham Clinton entered the White House as First Lady. Clinton researchers and political opponents sought out the thesis, thinking it contained evidence that Rodham had held strong radical or socialist views.

In early 1993, the White House requested that Wellesley not release the thesis to anyone. Wellesley complied, instituting a new rule that closed access to the thesis of any sitting U.S. president or first lady, a rule that in practice applied only to Rodham. Clinton critics and several biographers seized upon this action as a sure sign that the thesis held politically explosive contents that would reveal her radicalism or extremism. Hostile Clinton biographer Barbara Olson wrote in 1999 that Clinton "does not want the American people to know the extent to which she internalized and assimilated the beliefs and methods of Saul Alinsky." In her 2003 memoirs, Clinton mentioned the thesis only briefly, saying she had agreed with some of Alinsky's ideas, but had not agreed with his belief that it was impossible to "change the system" from inside.

Years after the Clintons left the White House, the mystery thesis held its allure; for example, in 2005 Clinton critic Peggy Noonan wrote that it was "the Rosetta Stone of Hillary studies ... [which] Wellesley College obligingly continues to suppress on her request."

In fact, however, the thesis had been unlocked after the Clintons left the White House in 2001 and is available for reading at the Wellesley College archives. In 2005, msnbc.com investigative reporter Bill Dedman sent his journalism class from Boston University to read the thesis and write articles about it; one of the students, Rick Heller, posted his article online in December 2005. The thesis is also available through interlibrary loan on microfilm, a method reporter Dorian Davis used when he obtained it in January 2007, and sent it to Noonan and to Clinton critic Amanda Carpenter at Human Events, who wrote a piece on it in March. Although publishing the thesis violates copyright, it can nevertheless be found on various websites.

The suppression of the thesis from 1993 to 2001 at the request of the Clinton White House was documented in March 2007 by reporter Dedman, who read the thesis at the Wellesley library and interviewed Rodham's thesis adviser. Dedman found that the thesis did not disclose Rodham's own views much. A Boston Globe assessment found the thesis nuanced, and said that "While [Rodham] defends Alinsky, she is also dispassionate, disappointed, and amused by his divisive methods and dogmatic ideology." Rodham's former professor and thesis adviser Alan Schechter told msnbc.com that "There Is Only The Fight . . ." was a good thesis, and that its suppression by the Clinton White House "was a stupid political decision, obviously, at the time." End.

What are Alinsky's rules from 'Rules for Radicals' that drew Hillary Clinton to his viewpoint of society? These are his 12 popular rules to destroy a society guided by Capitalism. His plans were only to destroy a society; never to change or improve a society.

Here is the complete list of rules from Alinsky:

* RULE 1: "Power is not only what you have, but what the enemy thinks you have." Power is derived from 2 main sources – money and people. "Have-Nots" must build power from flesh and blood.

* RULE 2: "Never go outside the expertise of your people." It results in confusion, fear and retreat. Feeling secure adds to the backbone of anyone.

* RULE 3: "Whenever possible, go outside the expertise of the enemy." Look for ways to increase insecurity, anxiety and uncertainty.

* RULE 4: "Make the enemy live up to its own book of rules." If the rule is that every letter gets a reply, send 30,000 letters. You can kill them with this because no one can possibly obey all of their own rules.

* RULE 5: "Ridicule is man's most potent weapon." There is no defense. It's irrational. It's infuriating. It also works as a key pressure point to force the enemy into concessions.

* RULE 6: "A good tactic is one your people enjoy." They'll keep doing it without urging and come back to do more. They're doing their thing, and will even suggest better ones

* RULE 7: "A tactic that drags on too long becomes a drag." Don't become old news.

* RULE 8: "Keep the pressure on. Never let up." Keep trying new things to keep the opposition off balance. As the opposition masters one approach, hit them from the flank with something new.

* RULE 9: "The threat is usually more terrifying than the thing itself." Imagination and ego can dream up many more consequences than any activist.

* RULE 10: "If you push a negative hard enough, it will push through and become a positive." Violence from the other side can win the public to your side because the public sympathizes with the underdog.

* RULE 11: "The price of a successful attack is a constructive alternative." Never let the enemy score points because you're caught without a solution to the problem.

* RULE 12: Pick the target, freeze it, personalize it, and polarize it." Cut off the support network and isolate the target from sympathy. Go after people and not institutions; people hurt faster than institutions.

Hillary Clinton, as indicated above, collaborated with Alinsky to form her early concepts of government and society. But, how has that association affected her more current ideas, policies and actions? Let's examine that question next.

Chapter 5
Hillary's New World

atriotupdate.com has a more current analysis of Hillary Clinton's political positions. This article by David L. Goetsch, on June 30, 2013, is titled: 'Who is worse for America: Barack Obama or Hillary Clinton?'

http://search.aol.com/aol/search?enabled_terms=&s_it=client97_sea
rchbox&q=Who+is+worse+for+America%3A+Barack+Obama+or+
Hillary+Clinton%3F%E2%80%99

"When Barack Obama squeaked by Hillary Clinton for the presidential nomination back in 2007, some conservatives sighed in relief and said, "Well at least Hillary won't be president," or words to that effect. Of course, when they made that kind of comment, they knew plenty about Hillary but relatively little about Obama. I wonder if conservatives would make this kind of comment today. The functional question is this: Who is worse for America, Barack Obama or Hillary Clinton? I know what you are thinking. Why not just ask if the reader would rather be run over by a truck or a bus? To paraphrase Hillary Clinton: What does it matter?

The reason I bring up this unwelcome topic is that even with Benghazi on her record and even with her subsequent testimony in which she insulted the grieving families of the Americans who were abandoned and killed in that God-forsaken place, Hillary is still the odds-on favorite to win the Democratic nomination for president. Provided she can stay out of jail over the Benghazi tragedy—and her record of legal slipperiness is well established—the next Republican candidate for the presidency will run against Hillary Clinton. Since this is the case, it behooves all Americans to consider Hillary's beliefs as demonstrated by her own words.

"We are going to take things away from you on behalf of the common good." These may sound like the words of Marx, Lenin, Stalin, or Mao (or Barack Obama for that matter), but they are the words of Hillary Clinton. She made this socialist statement all the way back in 2004, well before Barack Obama introduced the concept of redistribution of wealth as a normal plank in the Democrat's political platform. In other words, Hillary was leaning toward socialism even before Barack Obama took up the cause. Don't forget, before there was Obamacare there was Hillarycare. When it comes to socialized medicine, Obama just finished what Hillary started.

In 2007, Hillary made it clear that her leftwing philosophy had not changed when she said: "We…can't just let business as usual go on, and that means something has to be taken away from some people." By "business as usual" Hillary meant free market economics in which people pursue opportunity, accept personal responsibility, work hard to build a better life, and enjoy individual and economic freedom. What red-blooded leftist would want this type of business as usual to go on? Not Marx, not Lenin, not Stalin, not Mao, and certainly not Hillary. The "something" that Hillary claimed must be taken away from "some people" is not just money in the form of coercive taxes but freedom—the very freedoms guaranteed in our Constitution.

In the same speech in 2007, Hillary also said: "We have to build a political consensus that requires people to give up a little of their own…in order to create this common ground." Quite a statement. Let's parse her words and see what Hillary really means. She talks about building a "political consensus" but what she really means is a voting majority. In order to pass coercive tax laws that require "people to give up a little of their own," Hillary and her comrades on the left will need a dependable voting majority consisting of people who will be on the receiving end when wealth is redistributed. After all, what sane person is going to willingly give up what he has worked hard to earn when the recipient is someone who not only has not worked hard, but does not intend to. In fact, not only do Hillary's fortunate recipients of other people's money not intend to work, they don't even think they should have to. It's called the entitlement mentality.

Barack Obama ranks right down there among the worst of America's presidents. He is right in there with James Buchanan, Warren Harding, Millard Fillmore, John Tyler, Andrew Johnson, Franklin Pierce, and even Jimmy Carter. But even so, I am afraid Hillary will be even worse, provided of course she can win the presidency. It may be hard to imagine things getting worse than they have been under Barack Obama, but I suspect Hillary could manage. End of article.

Discoverthenetworks.org offered an over-all analysis of Hillary Clinton's background and history. These are some important points from that analysis:

1. Rodham was deeply influenced by a 1966 article titled "Change or Containment," which appeared in Motive, a magazine for college-age Methodists. Authored by the Marxist/Maoist theoretician Carl Oglesby, who was a leader of the Students for a Democratic Society, this piece defended Ho Chi Minh, Fidel Castro, and Maoist tactics of violence. Its thesis was that "certain cultural settings" (most notably American capitalism) were inherently inequitable and oppressive, and thus caused people to feel "pain and rage" that sometimes erupted into violence -- like that of "the rioters in Watts or Harlem" -- which was "reactive and provoked" rather than aggressive or malicious. Hillary later said that the Motive article had played a key role in her metamorphosis from Goldwater Republican in 1964 to leftist

Democrat in 1968. During her years as First Lady of the United States, Mrs. Clinton would tell a Newsweek reporter that she still treasured the Oglesby piece.

2. Following the June 1968 assassination of Democratic presidential hopeful Robert F. Kennedy, Hillary ended her affiliation with the Wellesley campus Young Republicans and volunteered in New Hampshire to work on the presidential campaign of antiwar candidate Eugene McCarthy. When McCarthy later dropped out of the Democratic primary, Hillary threw her support behind the Party's eventual nominee, Hubert Humphrey. From that point forward, wrote Barbara Olson in her 1999 book Hell to Pay, "Republicans were the enemy and the enemy was allied with evil -- the evils of war, racism, sexism, and poverty."

3. At Yale, Hillary was strongly influenced by the radical theoretician Duncan Kennedy, founder of the academic movement known as critical legal studies, which, drawing on the works of the Frankfurt School, viewed law as a "social construct" that corrupt power structures routinely exploited as an instrument of oppression to protect and promote their own bourgeois values at the expense of the poor and disenfranchised. Advocates of critical legal studies were interested in revolutionary change and the building of a new society founded on Marxist principles.

4. Hillary served as one of nine editors of the Yale Review of Law and Social Action, where she worked collaboratively with Mickey Kantor (who, more than two decades later, would serve as U.S. Trade Representative and U.S. Commerce Secretary under President Bill Clinton) and Robert Reich (who would serve as Bill Clinton's Labor Secretary from 1993 to 1997). "For too long," said the Yale Review, "legal issues have been defined and discussed in terms of academic doctrine rather than strategies for social change." The publication was replete with articles by or about such radicals as William Kunstler,

Charles Reich (author of The Greening of America); Jerry Rubin (who wrote a piece exhorting parents to "get high with our seven-year-olds," and urging students to "kill our parents"); and Charles Garry (the civil rights attorney who defended Black Panther Party members accused of murder). The Fall and Winter 1970 editions of the Yale Review, on which Hillary worked as associate editor, focused heavily on the trials of Black Panthers who had been charged with murder. Numerous cartoons in those issues depicted police officers as hominid pigs.

5. One of Hillary's Yale professors, Thomas Emerson (known as "Tommy the Commie"), introduced her to the aforementioned Charles Garry. Garry helped Hillary get personally involved in the defense of several Black Panthers (including the notorious Bobby Seale) who were then being tried in New Haven, Connecticut for the torture, murder, and mutilation of one of their own members. Though evidence of the defendants' guilt was overwhelming, Hillary -- as part of her coursework for Professor Emerson -- attended the Panther trials and arranged for shifts of fellow students to likewise monitor court proceedings and report on any civil-rights abuses allegedly suffered by the defendants. (Those abuses could then be used, if the Panthers were to lose their case, as grounds for appeal.) Striving to neutralize what she considered the pervasive racism of the American legal system, "Hillary was," as Barbara Olson observed in Hell to Pay, "a budding Leninist."

6. Also in 1972, she went to Berkeley to work as an intern at her hand-picked law firm: Treuhaft, Walker, and Bernstein. Founded by current or former members of the Communist Party USA, this firm had long acted as a legal asset not only for the CPUSA but also for the Black Panthers and other Bay-area radicals. Founding partner Bob Treuhaft, head of the California Communist Party, had been labeled one of the nation's most "dangerously subversive" lawyers. According to historian Stephen Schwartz, "Treuhaft is a man who dedicated his entire legal career to advancing the agenda of the Soviet Communist

Party and the KGB." Hillary did yeoman's work while learning at the feet of Treuhaft and his fellow masters. Associates say that Hillary, during her tenure with the firm, helped draftees get themselves declared conscientious objectors so they could avoid serving in Vietnam; they also contend that Hillary served VA interns seeking to avoid taking a loyalty oath to the United States.

7. Edelman went on to help Hillary secure a coveted research position with the Carnegie Council on Children, where the young attorney assisted Yale psychology professor Kenneth Keniston in the production of a report (titled All Our Children) advocating a dramatic expansion of social-welfare entitlements and a national guaranteed income -- all in the name of children's rights. Moreover, the report maintained that the traditional nuclear family was not inherently preferable to any other family structure, and that society had an obligation to honor, encourage, and support alternate arrangements such as single-parent households. What really mattered, said the Council, was the network of professionals -- teachers, pediatricians, social workers, and day-care workers -- who would collectively play the most vital role in raising children properly. In short, the Carnegie Council preached that childrearing was less a parental matter than a societal task to be overseen by "public advocates" -- judges, bureaucrats, social workers and other "experts" in childrearing -- who could intervene between parents and children on the latter's behalf. According to the report, the role of parents should be subordinate to the role of these experts.

8. Viewing America as an authoritarian, patriarchal, male-dominated society that tended to oppress women, children, and minorities, Hillary wrote a November 1973 article for the Harvard Educational Review advocating the liberation of children from "the empire of the father." She claimed that the traditional nuclear family structure often undermined the best interests of children, who "consequently need social institutions specifically designed to safeguard their position."

"Along with the family," she elaborated, "past and present examples of such arrangements include marriage, slavery, and the Indian Reservation system." She added: "Decisions about motherhood and abortion, schooling, cosmetic surgery, treatment of venereal disease, or employment, and others where the decision or lack of one will significantly affect a child's future should not be made unilaterally by parents."

9. Decades later, Hillary would take up these themes again in her 1996 book It Takes a Village, which stressed the importance of the larger community of adults -- many of whom are paid caretakers whose labors are funded by American taxpayers -- in childrearing.

10. Bill Clinton served as Governor of Arkansas from 1978 to 1980, and again from 1982 to 1992. Thus Mrs. Clinton spent a total of twelve years as Arkansas's First Lady. During that time, she continued her legal practice as a partner in the Rose Law Firm. In 1978 she became a board member of the Children's Defense Fund (CDF), and from 1986 to 1992 she served as chair of the CDF Board. From 1982 to 1988 Mrs. Clinton also chaired the New World Foundation (NWF), which had helped to launch CDF in 1973. During her years at NWF's helm, the Foundation made grants to such organizations as the National Lawyers Guild, the Institute for Policy Studies, the Christic Institute, Grassroots International, the Committees in Solidarity with the People of El Salvador (which sought to foment a Communist revolution in Central America), and groups with ties to the most extreme elements of the African National Congress.

11. In the spring of 1993, shortly after her husband took his oath of office, Mrs. Clinton delivered the commencement address at the University of Texas. In her speech, she stated: "We are at a stage in history in which remolding society is one of the great challenges facing all of us in the West."

12. That same year, Mrs. Clinton latched onto the phrase "the politics of meaning," an opaque concept coined by Michael Lerner that blended radical politics with New Ageish human potentialism. She invited Lerner to the White House, briefly making him her "guru" until the ridicule which this caused made her retreat from the connection. (In her autobiography, Mrs. Clinton strenuously avoids any mention of Lerner, or of Lerner's Tikkun magazine.)

13. Also during her early years as First Lady, Mrs. Clinton was put in charge of the 500-member Health Care Task Force which tried, in secret meetings and by stealth, to socialize medical care in the United States, a sector that represented approximately one-seventh of the U.S. economy. This modus operandi was in violation of so-called "sunshine laws," which forbid such secret meetings from taking place when non-government employees are present. Mrs. Clinton was sued by the Association of American Physicians and Surgeons for these violations. The trial judge, U.S. District Judge Royce C. Lamberth, ultimately ruled against her and the Clinton administration. In December 1997 Lamberth issued a 19-page report condemning as "reprehensible" the duplicity exhibited by Mrs. Clinton's Task Force. "The Executive Branch of the government, working in tandem, was dishonest with this court, and the government must now face the consequences of its misconduct," said Lamberth. "It is clear," he added, "that the decisions here were made at the highest levels of government. There were no rogue lawyers here misleading the court."

The linchpin of Mrs. Clinton's healthcare plan was a mandate forcing all Americans to purchase insurance, and imposing a penalty on those who failed to comply. In November 2013, MIT professor John Gruber, who was a chief architect of the Patient Protection & Affordable Care Act (Obamacare), said that Hillary Clinton's 1990s-era plan was "much more interventionist" than Obamacare, "much to the left of Obamacare," and "would have more radically changed our healthcare system."

14. During the 1990s, Mrs. Clinton spent eight years faithfully attending Foundry United Methodist Church in Washington, D.C., which was then pastored by the Rev. Dr. J. Philip Wogaman. Wogaman had made his political worldview clear in his many writings and sermons over the years. For instance, in 1990, a year after the fall of the Berlin Wall, he wrote that "Christian socialism's critique of the excesses and brutalities and idolatries of the free market still need to be heard." On an earlier occasion, he had lauded the "modest but real economic success" of Communist Cuba and China. As long ago as 1967, Wogaman had written: "The USSR is characteristic of the more tolerant Communist arrangements for religion. In Russia there are specific constitutional guarantees of freedom of worship, and some provision has even been made for the upkeep of churches and theological seminaries."

By no means was Wogaman the only radical cleric to be admired by Mrs. Clinton. In her 2004 memoir, Living History, Mrs. Clinton praised Rev. William Sloane Coffin Jr., who had served as Yale's chaplain during Hillary's years at the law school, for his "articulate moral critique of American involvement" in Vietnam. That critique involved his traveling to Hanoi in 1972. Seven years later, he would make a friendly trip to Tehran, capital of the first modern Islamic theocratic state which had just stormed a U.S. embassy and kidnapped dozens of his fellow countrymen.

15. Hillary's Nasty, Disrespectful Treatment of Secret Service & Military Personnel: In his 2014 book The First Family Detail, bestselling author Ronald Kessler writes that during Mrs. Clinton's years as First Lady, she was known and despised by Secret Service agents and military personnel for the nasty treatment, explosive temper, and imperious attitude she conveyed toward them. "Agents say being on Hillary Clinton's detail is the worst duty assignment in the Secret Service," writes Kessler. "Being assigned to her detail is a form of punishment." In August 2014, the Daily Mail provided the

following details from Kessler's book:

"We were basically told, the Clintons don't want to see you, they don't want to hear you, get out of the way,' according to a former Secret Service agent."

"She didn't like law enforcement officers or the military, former Secret Service agent Lloyd Bulman stated. 'She was just really rude to almost everybody. She'd act like she didn't want you around, like you were beneath her.' She went years without speaking to some agents."

"In response to a cheerful 'Good morning, ma'am,' by a former uniformed officer, Hillary's response to him was 'F--k off.'"

"While publicly courting law enforcement organizations, privately she felt disdain. She wanted state troopers and local police to wear suits and drive unmarked cars. No military aides could wear their uniforms in the White House. If agents driving her went over a bump, she'd swear at them."

"Glad-handing on the road on her Senatorial campaign, when they arrived at a 4-F Club in the land of dairy cows in upstate New York, she saw cows and people in jeans. That enraged her and she asked a staffer, 'What the f*** did we come her for? There's no money here.'"

"White House deputy counsel Vince Foster, who committed suicide in June 1993, was on the receiving end of a virulent verbal attack by Hillary. She disagreed with a legal opinion he made and humiliated him in a meeting, stating he would never be more than a hick-town lawyer and wasn't ready for the big time. 'The put-down that she gave him in that big meeting just pushed him over the edge', [former FBI agent Coy] Copeland says. She blamed Foster for all of the Clinton's problems and stated he had failed the couple...."

16. Analysis of Hillary's Worldview and Agendas:

"Hillary Clinton's alliances with organizations like CAP, MMFA, and ACS serve as indicators of her most deeply held political beliefs and objectives. David Horowitz has provided the following incisive analysis of Mrs. Clinton's broad agendas and the tactics she employs in pursuit of them:

"It is possible to be a socialist, and radical in one's agendas, and yet moderate in the means one regards as practical to achieve them. To change the world, it is first necessary to acquire cultural and political power. And these transitional goals may often be accomplished by indirection and deception even more effectively than by frontal assault. ... New Left progressives [such as] Hillary Clinton ... [share the] intoxicating vision of a social redemption achieved by Them ... For these self-appointed social redeemers, the goal -- 'social justice' -- is not about rectifying particular injustices, which would be practical and modest, and therefore conservative. Their crusade is about rectifying injustice in the very order of things. 'Social Justice' for them is about a world reborn, a world in which prejudice and violence are absent, in which everyone is equal and equally advantaged and without fundamentally conflicting desires. It is a world that could only come into being through a re-structuring of human nature and of society itself. ... In other words, a world in which human consciousness is changed, human relations refashioned, social institutions transformed, and in which 'social justice' prevails. ... In short, the transformation of the world requires the permanent entrenchment of the saints in power. Therefore, everything is justified that serves to achieve the continuance of them. ... The focus of Hillary Clinton's ambition ... is the vision of a world that can only be achieved when the Chosen accumulate enough power to change this one." End of discoverthenetworks article.

Perhaps anyone planning to, or thinking about supporting Hillary

Rodham Clinton for any future political office should consider many things before they make that decision. In making that decision there are three important questions:

1. What is my vision for the future of my country, and my descendants: my children, grandchildren and all who come after?

2. Will Hillary Clinton or anyone who promotes the socialistic philosophies that she does, lead our great nation toward that vision?

3. Will I want future generations to look back on history and ask; "Were those who supported that Communist/Socialist agenda simply non-thinking 'Useful Idiots?'"

Finally, Hillary claims to care so greatly about women. Does she, really, or is she just pandering for votes? Read the information at this link and decide for yourself. She defended a rapist against a 12 year old girl, then laughed about it after she discredited the girl and helped the rapist escape a penalty.

http://www.thedailybeast.com/articles/2014/06/20/exclusive-hillary-clinton-took-me-through-hell-rape-victim-says.html

So far in this discussion, Hillary Clinton's background, training, and social inclinations have been explained and exposed. Therefore, would it be reasonable for her to pick one of her kind to be her vice presidential running mate? Or would she choose someone who might be considered more moderate, and in line with clear patriotic choices; rejecting that danger pressing upon us from that hidden and silent jihad? It seems Tim Kaine might be influenced by the same tendencies as Hillary.

Chapter 6
Islam Bores Deeper

In his article titled, 'Dem VP Tim Kaine: Another Islamist Sympathizer In the White House,' George Rasley, CHQ Editor wrote this 7/27/2016, as reported at this link:

http://www.conservativehq.com/node/23685

"In our articles "Is Huma Abedin Hillary Clinton's Alger Hiss?" and "Yes, the Muslim Penetration of America Is Real" and "Why Ben Carson Is Right - No Muslim Should Be President Of the United States" we documented that anti-constitutional Muslim Brotherhood sympathizers and agents of influence have penetrated Hillary Clinton's State Department staff and political operation.

And through their Freedom of Information Act requests and related lawsuits our friends at Judicial Watch have uncovered that Muslim Brotherhood-connected Clinton aide Huma Abedin was at the very center of the massive security breach caused by Mrs. Clinton's private email server.

But what has received less attention are the documented two-decade-long ties between Democratic vice presidential nominee Senator Tim Kaine and Muslim Brotherhood operatives and front groups.

Virginia is a hotbed of Islamism in America and Kaine, Virginia's former Governor and now junior Senator, has received thousands of

Hillary Clinton: To Destroy a Nation   Will Clark

dollars in contributions from individuals associated with the Islamic Society of North America (ISNA) and the Council on American-Islamic Relations (CAIR), both unindicted co-conspirators in the Holy Land Foundation for Relief and Development (HLF) case– the largest terror-funding trial in U.S. history.

Kaine likewise has ties to Jamal al Barzinji, an Iraqi-born businessman and founder of the Islamic Society of North America and the International Institute of Islamic Thought (IIIT) which was also demonstrated by the Justice Department to be an unindicted coconspirator in the HLF case.

All told, Kaine received more than $43,000 from the New Dominion PAC, a front for various Islamist groups, including the International Institute of Islamic Thought which donated $10,000 to the PAC.

Likewise, Breitbart reports that the Middle East Forum's Islamist Money in Politics database shows another $4,300 donated to Kaine's Senate campaign in 2011-2012 by officials from Islamic Society of North America (ISNA) and the Council on American-Islamic Relations (CAIR). Another $3,500 came from Hisham Al-Talib, a leader from Barzinji's IIIT organization.

Kaine of course defends his Islamist friends or pleads ignorance of his friends and supporters' ties to the Muslim Brotherhood and Islamist terrorist organizations, but their ties are so public and so deep that only *willful blindness* could leave Tim Kaine in doubt about how dangerous his friends are to constitutional liberty.

As our friend former Assistant U.S. Attorney, and Islamist terrorist prosecutor, Andrew C. McCarthy documented in his article for National Review, "International Institute of Islamic Thought and the Muslim Brotherhood" there is abundant evidence tying the

94

International Institute of Islamic Thought to the Muslim Brotherhood and its agenda:

To begin with, the Brotherhood is prominently cited in DOJ's coconspirator list for the HLF case. More significantly, central to the HLF prosecution was the Brotherhood's 1991 internal memorandum, discussed in my column. The IIIT is expressly identified by the Muslim Brotherhood in that memorandum as being among "our organizations and the organizations of our friends." In addition, IIIT board members Jamal Barzinji and Yaqub Mirza have been identified in an FBI investigation as leading members of the Muslim Brotherhood. Barzinji is also listed as secretary-general of the Islamic Society of North America (ISNA). As noted in my column, ISNA is specifically cited as coconspirator by the Justice Department. Moreover, Sayyid Syeed, a founder of IIIT, was also a founder of the ISNA. Syeed has also served on the board of advisers of the Council for American Islamic Relations (CAIR), which is also cited in the Justice Department's HLF coconspirator list.

IIIT board member Barzinji was also a co-founder of the Muslim Students Association that was later merged into ISNA. Abdel Rahman Alamoudi is a close associate of Barzinji's. As the Hudson Institute's Zeyno Baran has recounted, when IIIT convinced the U.S. government to allow IIIT to be "the official arbiters of Islam in the U.S. military," Alamoudi was tasked to select Muslim chaplains for American armed forces. Alamoudi, who has been probed in the Justice Department's investigations of the IIIT and Sami al-Arian, was later convicted for illegal transactions with the Libyan government and assisting in a plot to assassinate then-Crown Prince Abdullah of Saudi Arabia.

Finally, as detailed in my column, the IIIT was a major contributor to al-Arian, a former Muslim Brotherhood member who was later convicted of terrorism charges arising out of his association with Palestinian Islamic Jihad (PIJ). PIJ has long been formally designated

95

as a foreign terrorist organization under U.S. law. IIIT cofounder and president, Shaykh Taha Jabir al-Awani, was cited by the Justice Department as unindicted coconspirator number 5 in the al-Arian case.

McCarthy's exposé of Barzinji, IIIT and their connection to the Muslim Brotherhood was published July 24, 2010 while Kaine was campaigning for the Senate and still taking money from individuals associated with Muslim Brotherhood front groups, such as CAIR, ISNA and IIIT.

Like Hillary Clinton, either through willful blindness or sympathy with its anti-western agenda, for almost two decades Tim Kaine has associated with and allowed himself to be penetrated by the Muslim Brotherhood and its front groups.

At a time when Islam's war against the West is reaching a crucial and increasingly violent phase, electing Hillary Clinton and Tim Kaine as President and Vice President, two individuals with documented ties to the Muslim Brotherhood and other Islamist front groups, amounts to national suicide.

George Rasley is editor of ConservativeHQ, a member of American MENSA and a veteran of over 300 political campaigns, including every Republican presidential campaign from 1976 to 2008. He served as lead advance representative for Governor Sarah Palin in 2008 and has served as a staff member, consultant or advance representative for some of America's most recognized conservative Republican political figures, including President Ronald Reagan and Jack Kemp. He served in policy and communications positions on the House and Senate staff, and during the George H.W. Bush administration he served on the White House staff of Vice President Dan Quayle."

Chapter 7
Islam and Satan

Most of the writing in this book has been to explain the danger of electing Hillary Clinton as the President of the United States. And, basically, the writings suggest that since she hates the traditional United States system of government, Capitalism, she plans to change it into something else; but she's not sure what. Perhaps she intends to move more toward pure Socialism, but her efforts are confused and complicated. Pandora's Box has been opened and out came the dangerous horrors of Islam; bumping Capitalism and Socialism out of the picture. Now, her actions seem to point toward her promoting and accepting that newer and more dangerous condition. Therefore, the discussion in this chapter will be focused on how and why Islam is such a threat to the United States, and to total humanity.

Remember from an earlier chapter I included this Bible reference explaining why we should not allow Muslims into our country? I will repeat it here for current reference:

Should we invite Muslims, who worship Satan, into our great nation, founded on Christian principles? Christ answers this question in 2 John, 9-11:

"Whosoever transgresseth, and abideth not in the doctrine of Christ, hath not God. He that abideth in the doctrine of Christ, he hath both the Father and the Son. If there come any unto you, and bring not this doctrine, receive him not into your house, and neither bid him God speed. For he that biddeth him God speed is partaker of his evil deeds."

Now, at this time, it's appropriate to ask another question; that is, 'why would God make such a pronouncement?' Aren't we told to 'love our neighbors, etc. etc.?' Now, I will answer these questions; but before I do I caution those who refuse to believe there is a real God, and He has a Son named Jesus Christ to close their eyes and put their hands over their ears. If their minds are so tightly sealed to reject God, then they will be offended by these next words – and might lose sleep for several weeks. So these next words of explanation are meant for those who believe; and for those others who might want to take a little peak with half-opened eyes just in case they consider changing their minds about God's existence. To those I say, be careful, for you might fall in.

Now, to explain why I am so involved with these interpretations and explanations. I was a casual reader of Revelation, in the Bible, before Barack Obama became president. When he became president, I knew it was something biblical, so I delved into it more trying to answer my question –why? Every day since that election, I have been reading in Revelation trying to understand, more and more. My first book about the danger of Obama was titled, 'The Day America Died.' That was immediately after his re-election in 2012. Since then, I've learned so much more from Revelation. Most people find it so confusing they don't even bother trying to read it. After all this time, I find it a fascinating story that's so clear. Even within Revelation, itself, it proclaims the message is 'crystal clear.' To demonstrate, let's interpret that message. It's self-contained in Chapter 4, Verse 6:

"And before the throne there was a sea of glass like unto crystal: and in the midst of the throne, and round about the throne, were four beasts full of eyes before and behind."

These were the four beasts who introduced the riders of the 'four horses of the apocalypse' in Chapter 6. These were the white horse, the red horse, the black horse and the pale horse. These riders are the actors in the full Revelation story. Understanding the results of their actions gives a complete understanding of the story in Revelation. That story is about Satan trying to remove God from Heaven. So, what about that 'crystal clear' comment in Chapter 4, Verse 6?

To begin, the word 'beast' in Revelation does not describe a beast, as we ordinarily consider that word. Instead, it also describes a presence or a condition. So, what that verse really means is that the 'presence of God could see in the past and into the future (eyes before and behind) in a sea of glass like crystal'. Or, He can see everything 'crystal clear.' Then He introduces the riders of the four horses in Chapter 6:

The white horse represents God and His forces. Those forces are later described as followers of God in the Spirit to repel Satan's attackers. The red horse is described as one who will take peace from the earth and that the one rider would kill one another. Islam is one religion that kills one another. The black horse describes commerce of the earth that will be devastated during the tribulation period. Commodities worldwide will become scarce or non-existent; Rich men of the sea (shipping commerce) shall weep. The rider that sat on the pale horse was Death, and Hell followed with him...'to kill with sword, and with hunger, and with death, and with the beasts of the earth.' Later this is described as death by war, hunger, thirst, and pestilence; when nothing is available to eat, drink, or defend against pests. In summary, these four horses represent the full story of Revelation; and as the other reference stated – crystal clear.

Okay, I can hear the doubters now saying there is nothing in the Bible that gives a clear reference to anything in the past or in the future; it's all a made-up story to scare everyone into 'turning to God.' Surprising

99

to many, yes there is a clear starting point that creates a time table to explain the other parts. It just takes a little research and cross-referencing to make it crystal clear. It begins in Chapter 12.

Basically, Chapter 12 presents the starting point to Revelation's story. The letters to the seven churches in Asia begin Revelation, but when all is considered those letters are not just to those seven churches. Those letters create the index, the table of contents, to the remainder of Revelation. That's explained in my other books, but that's not the purpose for this part of this book. The purpose here is to make these specific points very clear and precise for those unsure and for those doubters; so everyone will understand the full danger of Islam to our security and to our future. So, let's continue and keep this as concise as possible.

Chapter 12 begins by announcing the appearance of two 'wonders' in heaven. The first was a 'great' wonder which represented the woman, Christianity; and another wonder (not a great wonder) which was the angel Satan. Then it describes the birth of Christ (the woman ready to be delivered.) It also says the dragon stood before the woman 'for to devour her child as soon as it was born.' This clearly represents Herod's attempt to kill Jesus in an effort called The Massacre of the Innocents. He failed. The next section explained that Satan had been removed from Heaven by Michael and his angels. Verse 13 says, "And when the dragon saw that he was cast unto the earth, he persecuted the woman (Christianity) which brought forth the man child (Christ.) So, what happened after much persecution of Christians by Jews and Romans? That persecution ended at a certain time and event. This is the only place in Revelation that allows times to be determined. The code to Revelation's message is deciphered through Verse 14:

"And to the woman (Christianity) were given two wings of a great eagle, that she might fly into the wilderness, into her place, where she is nourished for a time, and times, and half a time, from the face of the serpent."

These stated times have real time and place meaning. Let's begin by understanding the 'two wings of a great eagle' that protected Christianity. It began on 28 October 312 A.D. at the Battle of the Milvian Bridge between the Roman Emperors Constantine and Maxentius. Constantine won that battle, and he had two items with him that he attributed to his victory. First was the usual battle staff that went before his marching troops. It was a high staff at the top of which had a bronze eagle with two prominent wings. But the most significant thing to which he attributed his victory was the Christian cross, which he had his men paint on their shields the night before the battle.

It began the day before the battle, just after noon. Constantine saw a cross of light in the heavens, just above the sun. It had on it the inscription 'Conquer By This.' Some say he claimed he had another vision during the night, a visitor who confirmed the interpretation of the first vision. He won that major battle the next day and became known as Constantine the 'Great.' His symbol was an eagle with outstretched wings. He continued to win more battles then consolidated Rome. Then he created the Roman Catholic Church approximately 350 A.D. His mother, Saint Helena, collected and protected many of the special Christian artifacts still remaining in Jerusalem at that time.

After that, Christianity, 'that woman,' was protected (nourished) for 'a time, and times, and half a time.' Using common rational thought that would mean 350 years (a hundred years plus 200 years plus 50 years.). Considering the first 350 years, until the establishment of the church, then 350 years of protection; that brings the time line to 700 A.D. What happened at that time? That's when Islam evolved; that's when Christianity was viciously attacked again. Or, as the last verse in Chapter 12, Verse 17 reveals:

"And the dragon was wroth with the woman, and went to make war with the remnant of her seed, which keep the commandments of God, and have the testimony of Jesus Christ."

In summary, Chapter 12 reveals the birth of Christ, and the woman, Christianity; and it also reveals the appearance of Satan to destroy Christianity when Satan was removed from Heaven by Michael and his angels. Then, when Satan failed to kill Christianity at its birth, he then became angrier (wroth) and continues to make war against all Christians, even today. That's the content of Chapter 12. But, the very important part of Chapter 12 is that it gives dates to confirm the events – that revelation. A recent speech by Hillary Clinton confirms Satan's continued war against Christians. That will be discussed later. For now, let's continue with Revelation's story.

As Chapter 12 gave the full introduction of Christ and Christianity; so also does Chapter 13 give the full introduction of Satan and his forces. The information about Satan and his forces is also crystal clear. This interpretation is a little longer than the information in Chapter 12, so for all those doubters taking a peek pretending to reject these prophesies; please have a little more patience. We are getting there.

Chapter 13 begins with a vision from Apostle John, the writer, saying he stood on the sand of the sea, to describe what he saw. This first statement, although seemingly innocuous, is more important than ordinarily gleaned. In many cases in Revelation the word 'sea' means the sea of humanity or the sea of people. John included the word 'sand' to indicate it was a real sea of water. Then he added that he saw seven heads and ten horns rise out of the sea, 'and upon his heads the name of blasphemy.' Many interpret these seven heads to indicate Rome, as in the seven hills of Rome, suggesting the old Roman Empire would return to become the 'beast' in Revelation. Some even propose the Pope is or will be the antichrist. In both suggestions nothing could be further from the truth.

The seven heads rising from the sea involving sand are the seven continents of the earth. The ten heads are the ten nations of the earth that will be the kingdoms of Islam. Islam creates that blasphemy by considering Muhammad superior to Jesus Christ. That's the full introduction. It explains who they are and what they believe. Then the next verses get even more specific if one gleans deeper seeking more clarity, and without having that biased built-in rejection of God. Come on, Atheists, Satan's warriors, and other doubters; stay with me as we continue.

Verse 2 says the dragon gave great authority to that beast with seven heads that rose from the sea. Then Verse 3 adds another comment that was later confirmed to fit the person, the time, and the situation. And remember; Revelation was written 700 years before the rise of Islam; before this described event:

"And I saw one of his heads as it were wounded to death; and his deadly wound was healed: and all the world wondered after the beast."

Some interpreters wrongly ascribe this comment to suggest the rise of the old Roman Empire that was dead. That's not the case. This is a verse that describes Muhammad, the founder of Islam. Muhammad was wounded with arrows to his face and his face was broken with rocks at the Battle of Uhud in 632 A.D. He fell 'as dead' on the battlefield and his troops retreated from the battle. He later 'rose from the dead' and joined them in their retreat.

Then Verse 4 says they, his followers, worshipped the dragon and they worshipped the beast given power by the dragon. This generic beast would include Islam as well as Muhammad. Verse 5 adds, "And there was given unto him (Muhammad) a mouth speaking great things and blasphemies; and power was given unto him to continue." Then Verse 6 specifically identifies Muhammad, "And he opened his mouth in blasphemy against God (denying that Jesus Christ was the Son of God) to blaspheme his name, and his tabernacle, and them that dwell in Heaven.

Now, this next verse creates the connection with the two identities, Islam and Christianity. Do you remember the words in Chapter 12, Verse 17 that begins, "And the dragon was wroth with the woman and went to make war with the remnant of her seed?" Chapter 13, Verse 7 makes that connection between Muhammad and Satan. It states:

"And it was given unto him to make war with the saints, and to overcome them: and power was given him over all kindreds and tongues, and nations." (Would this not include those seven continents that rose from the sea?)

Essentially, this says that Muhammad (Islam) was given power by Satan to war against God and His followers. But, why would Satan have such animosity against God, Christ, and all believers? That's also easy to explain by following and connecting the Words. Again, He makes it crystal clear.

Let's begin by referring to Chapter 12, Verse 9 after Satan's battle with Michael and his angels in Heaven:

"And the great dragon was cast out, that old serpent, called the Devil, and Satan, which deceiveth the whole world (those seven continents) he was cast out into the earth, and his angels were cast out with him."

What happened when Satan was cast out of Heaven? That's also explained in Chapter 10. This chapter begins by describing a mighty angel who came down from Heaven, holding a 'little book' in his hand. John heard words from that little book and started to write them, but was told by a voice from Heaven to 'write them not.' Then the angel who had come down from Heaven lifted his hand to Heaven, and in Verse 6 threatened to terminate God:

"And sware by him that liveth for ever and ever, who created heaven, and the things that therein are, and the earth, and the things that therein are, and the sea, and the things which are therein, that there should be time no longer." In summary, when Satan was kicked out of Heaven, he swore to God he would get his revenge and end God's time in Heaven.

Now, what about the words in that little book that John was told not to write? That little book is also very important, for the words from that little book are the words given to Muhammad and his followers to create their Koran. John's story continues in Verse 8:

"And the voice which I heard from Heaven spake unto me again, and said, Go and take the little book which is open in the hand of the angel (Satan) which standeth upon the sea and upon the earth." Verse 9, "Take it, and eat it up; and it shall make thy belly bitter, but it shall be in thy mouth sweet as honey." Verse 10 gives the conclusion, "And I took the little book out of the angel's hand and ate it up; and it was in my mouth sweet as honey: and as soon as I had eaten it, my belly was bitter."

Does this little book not describe Islam? Islam claims to be a religion of peace (honey) but the results of that Satan's religion are deadly and murderous (bitter.)

Thus far we have revealed Satan's connection and power over Islam. And, the antichrist Muhammad has been identified in Chapter 13, but even more is revealed in that chapter. It continues, explaining the death of Muhammad and the rise of the second beast to take his place. That begins in Verse 9:

"If any man have an ear, let him hear. 10) He that leadeth into captivity shall go into captivity: he that killeth with the sword must be killed with the sword. Here is the patience and the faith of the saints."

This describes the death of Muhammad – by the sword. Although he didn't die literally from a sword, he didn't die a natural death. He was poisoned by one of his captured wives. It was her revenge for Muhammad having killed her husband and her brother during one of his raids. Does this really describe the life of a real prophet; or a prophet of Satan?

The remainder of Chapter 13 then introduces and describes the actions of the second beast, also known as the False Prophet, who "Had two horns like a lamb, and he spake as a dragon." He claimed to be a Christian, but his praise was for Islam. Only one person, today, fits that description. That person is Barack Hussein Obama. The last verse, 18, gives a description of this person:

"Here is wisdom. Let him that hath understanding count the number of the beast: for it is the number of a man; and his number is Six hundred threescore and six." (666)

God's instruction is to count the number of the beast, so let's do that; 6+6+6 equals 18. So 18 is the number of the man's name. That would indicate his name is made of 18 letters. I wonder who that might be. Certainly that wouldn't suggest BARACKHUSSEINOBAMA; who claims to be a Christian, but who praises only Muhammad. So, you don't think that number 18 is correct? Then, why is that number confirmed by being presented and explained in Verse **18**?

There are many more ties and connections in Revelation that reveal the real and true story that Islam is Satan's religion to defeat God's religion and 'for God in Heaven there should be time no longer.' There are many; but for brevity, let's analyze just one more. That involves the woman Jezebel and the city Babylon.

Okay, you Atheists and doubters, you might want to open your eyes and ears fully on this one. It might not knock your shoes off, but it will certainly tug at your shirt tails to maybe let the concepts sink in just a little – especially if you might be somewhat concerned about your salvation in the hereafter. So, here goes.

It begins with that one rider of the red horse that 'goes forth to kill one another.' How can that happen; how can one rider kill one another? This is a connection in Chapter 2 that's answered in Chapter 17. In John's letter to the church at Thyatira (all churches of all times) the full information begins in Verse 20:

"Notwithstanding I have a few things against thee, because thou sufferest that woman Jezebel, which calleth herself a prophetess, to teach and to seduce my servants to commit fornication and to eat things sacrificed unto idols. 22) Behold, I will cast her into a bed, and them that commit adultery with her into great tribulation, except they repent of their deeds. 23) And I will kill her children with death; and all the churches shall know that I am he which searcheth the reins and hearts; and I will give unto every one of you according to your works." This letter ends, as do all seven letters, with the admonishment, "He that hath an ear, let him hear what the Spirit saith unto the churches."

As we progress in this interpretation, please keep two statements in mind: 'I will cast her into a bed,' and 'I will kill her children with death.' Before we go into Chapter 17 however, let's get more of Jezebel's identity. Remember, Jezebel 'calleth herself a prophetess.'

The letter to Ephesus begins that idea of false prophets. It's stated in Verse 2, "…and thou hast tried them which say they are apostles, and are not, and hast found them liars." That false prophet concept continues in the second letter, to Smyrna, Verse 9, "…and I know the blasphemy of them which say they are Jews, and are not, but are the synagogue of Satan." Then the letter to Philadelphia adds in Verse 9, "Behold, I will make them of the synagogue of Satan, which say they are Jews, and are not, but do lie; behold I will make them to come and worship before thy feet, and to know that I have loved thee."

In summary, these letters reveal the great falseness of Islam. First, Jezebel claims to be a prophetess (prophet) but is not. That false prophet represents Muhammad. The other references to the claim that they are Jews and apostles 'but are not' refer to Islam's claim that they are descended from the Jew, Abraham through Ishmael. They claim to be one of the three Abrahamic religions. They are not. The times of the Jewish tribes and the Arabic tribes in that area at that time do not allow for this connection. Even Muhammad said he couldn't go back except for 17 ancestries in his family, which did not include Jews. This can be confirmed by online inquiry. All this pertinent information is in some of my other books focusing on this subject. But, for now let's advance to Chapter 17 for the connecting information. Okay doubters, please follow along fully awake.

Chapter 17 opens with an angel telling John he would show him 'the judgment of the great whore that sitteth upon many waters: with whom the kings of the earth have committed fornication.' This is the same 'whore' Jezebel that was 'cast into a bed' with those to commit fornication. This was the result of God's promise. Then, her description, in Verse3, connected her as the rider of that red horse:

"So he carried me away in the spirit into the wilderness: and I saw a woman sit upon a scarlet colored beast (red horse) full of names of blasphemy, having seven heads and ten horns."

Does this description sound familiar? Then Verses 5 and 6 reveal who she is, what she is and her goal. Jezebel gets another name:

"And upon her forehead was a name written, Mystery, Babylon the Great, the Mother of Harlots and Abominations of the Earth. And I saw the woman drunken with the blood of the saints, and with the blood of the martyrs of Jesus."

This woman, Babylon the Great, (Islam in total) is fulfilling that task required and appointed by Satan in his quest to eliminate God from Heaven. Who else, in the whole world, besides Islam is 'drunken with the blood of the saints and with the blood of the martyrs of Jesus?' Muslims slaughter Christians and Jews at every opportunity and in any situation. Furthermore, if they were descendants of Jews, as they claim, why would they be waging such atrocities against Jews and Christians? In the words of Revelation: it's blasphemy.

Now, let's consider those comments about that one rider of the red horse killing one another; and about God's promise to kill Jezebel's children, who do not repent. Those two ideas are also revealed in this chapter. How does that happen? This is answered in Verses 16 through 18, as the angel keeps explaining to John:

"And the ten horns which thou sawest upon the beast, these shall hate the whore (the ten formal Islamic nations will hate the radicals) and shall make her desolate and naked, and shall eat her flesh, and burn her with fire. For God hath put in their hearts to fulfill his will, and to agree, and give their kingdom unto the beast, until the words of God shall be fulfilled. And the woman which thou sawest is that great city, which reigneth over the kings of the earth."

God said he would kill Jezebel's children, and the rider of the red horse was destined to kill one another. These acts are being fulfilled every day, every single day, by Muslims killing other Muslims. They are doing it themselves; through the will of God.

So now, it should be clear to everyone, even those extreme doubters, that the Word of God lives. It was prophesied to happen over two thousand years ago. Islam formed about 700 years after these words were written, and they are being fulfilled today; every day.

The other parts of Revelation are equally clear, but to explain those parts is not the purpose for this book. Those concepts are detailed in many of my other books regarding Revelation; many which are free. The purpose for this writing is to reveal that Barack Obama's extreme promotion of inviting many Muslims into our nation is a threat to destroy America.

Hillary Clinton's close support and comfort to Muslims, and her anxious invitation to invite many more into America is her open invitation for them to destroy the America we have enjoyed for so many generations. Certainly, they are 'peaceful' so long as there are only a few as our neighborly citizens. But once their numbers reach that dangerous level, America will be no more. Hillary Clinton will have done her part in fulfilling Satan's promise to destroy God's time in Heaven.

Conclusion

Hillary Clinton hopes to replace Obama as President of the United States. And, as with Obama, her goals seem very oriented against fulfilling those hopes and dreams of our Founding Fathers. In fact, her plans and ambitions for America seem in total opposition to those rights and opportunities our Founding Fathers planned for us. They planned personal freedom, individual opportunity for success and achievement, and fulfillment of human aspirations. Words from her mouth suggest a different plan for America; a plan that supports Obama's current agenda.

Her words propose an all-powerful central government that would determine and limit personal dreams and aspirations. The plans, rules and laws she propose are to take from the rich and redistribute to the poor. To the poor, this plan obviously sounds great. Isn't it nice to be promised something without any attachments or requirement to earn it? Just relax and enjoy life and let the government do everything for you. Although the parts sound great to many uninspired people; the results are always destructive. The government takes over stronger and stronger until nothing can be done in a nation without the government's approval or involvement. This may be understood from that quote at the beginning of this book, as Winston read from that book chapter, *Ignorance is Strength.* George Orwell's novel, 1984, was inspired by that early Socialist experiment in Russia.

That Socialist experiment began in full in Russia. It was the 'rise of the proletariat' the working class guided by Vladimir Lenin and his cohorts Carl Marx and others. Soon thereafter, the economy totally collapsed. Many citizens who were promised better lives through those actions died from starvation and pestilence. Many other millions were killed and imprisoned by those in charge; those same leaders who promised a better life for everyone.

A more current example of the failure of socialism is in Venezuela. That country is now in total chaos with many starving. The grocery shelves are all empty except for the very few; those in charge and those close to those in charge. Yes; they are living the life of 'free stuff' but there is not enough free stuff to satisfy everyone. This is an example of the life Hillary Clinton promises. But, her plans could make things even worse. Following Saul Alinsky's plan, there is only a plan to destroy our nation; without something positive to replace it; just destruction.

As I dream of the past, I wonder what we have done to ourselves. What has happened to this great nation established by our Founding Fathers? They fought; they gave their all to leave to us a nation of freedom, individual opportunity and a foundation upon which we are allowed to inspire our children and all those who follow us to see only goodness and progress into the future. They fought and died to give us that. They sacrificed all. Then during WWII thousands of brave Americans gave their lives and their futures to allow us to advance what our Founding Fathers planned for us. I remember it well. I was six years old when that war ended and the newspapers read in half page letters 'WAR ENDS.' Of course, I couldn't read at that time, but I knew those big words on the newspapers were something very important. What they actually said was 'America is great.'

I began school in 1945, the year the war ended. Then, and for the next decade, America was filled with hope, exhilaration, and high expectation that our nation was a nation under God, blessed by God, and protected by God. Then it was clear to almost everyone; God was our savior and protector, and most of us worshiped Him. We had no doubt God had saved the world from deadly and hell fire destruction by giving the world victory over that evil trying to destroy the world. But, what was most important at that time was that those who didn't worship God did not try to prove He did not exist. They chose to worship God, or not to worship God, but there was no great reason for them to change our ideas of God and religion. In other words, they didn'try to 'destroy' God and His power. Their belief was, in most part, kept personal to themselves. Today, that is no longer true. Today the dedicated aim of the forces of Islam is to destroy God; and replace him with their god, Satan.

Although the Words tell us not to invite those who worship Satan 'into our house' Barack Obama and Hillary Clinton continue to praise Islam; and strive to bring more of them into our great nation to further contaminate our society with that blasphemy. The more they invite them into our home, the greater becomes our peril to suffer great and horrible consequences. He has told us so; He has warned us. Yet, Barack Obama and Hillary Clinton continue to serve the goals and aims of Satan. That admonition comes from Second John, Verses 7-11:

"For many deceivers are entered into the world, who confess not that Jesus Christ is come in the flesh. This is a deceiver and an antichrist. Look to yourselves, that we lose not those things which we have wrought, but that we receive a full reward. Whosoever transgresseth, and abideth not in the doctrine of Christ, hath not God. He that abideth in the doctrine of Christ, he hath both the Father and the Son. If there come any unto you, and bring not this doctrine, receive him not into your house, neither bid him God speed. For he that biddeth him God speed is partaker of his evil deeds."

Hillary Clinton's intent to remove the worship of God in our wonderful nation was clearly, and likely accidentally, revealed in her keynote address at the 2015 Women in the World Summit in New

York. In that speech she said, "deep-seated cultural codes, religious beliefs and structural biases have to be changed" so that women can have access to "reproductive health care."

Is she actually suggesting that deep-seated religious beliefs have to be changed? And what does she suggest about those changes. Can one who believes in God believe in God if that person decides not to believe in God? Many people believe that killing a fetus in a womb is murder; it's killing a person. If one believes in God, then decides to agree with Hillary that they should change their mind about murder, that it's okay; can they still claim salvation under God? Since she is proposing that people of God should not adhere to God's Word, then it must be understood that she, herself, is not a person who respects or worships God.

Once again, this confirms her Pandora's Box paradigm. To dismiss God from a society is to dismiss a cohesive society; and invite in all the Devils anxious to replace that cohesive society. The Devil anxious and waiting is that one named Satan. From her actions and comments, Hillary has already adorned herself into his waiting and anxious arms. His soldiers of Islam are already sneaking into America through every crawly space.

Two other purposes of Revelation, other than to reveal Satan's oath to eliminate God's time in Heaven, are to assure Christians that God and His forces will win in the end; to hold fast and not get discouraged. In the end, nations will still exist and will be healed by 'leaves' from the tree of life. (Revelation 22:2) But, during the tribulation period before that ending there will be great hardships to endure. These will include death by the sword, starvation, thirst and pestilence. (Revelation 6:8) We are warned to 'prepare' and not be surprised or embarrassed by our nakedness of not being ready when those tribulations begin. (Revelation 16:15) That tribulation period will begin in the midst of that covenant affecting Israel. It's that covenant promoted by that false prophet, Barack Hussein Obama. It's the covenant that will be abandoned by Iran 'in the midst of that covenant,' and Israel will be savagely attacked. This is announced in Daniel 9:27:

"And he (probably the False Prophet) shall confirm the covenant with many for one week (seven years): and in the midst of the week he shall cause the sacrifice and the oblation to cease, and for the overspreading of abominations he shall make it desolate, even until the consummation, and that determined shall be poured upon the desolate."

This is generally interpreted as the beginning of the 'Abomination of Desolation,' the time that Jerusalem will be made desolate from an abomination placed there. That agreement (covenant) with Iran regarding their nuclear capability was signed in July, 2015.

'In the midst' is not a definitive time. If that means 'in the middle' then it would begin three and a half years after the covenant was signed. However, 'in the midst' could mean anytime within that seven year period. We must assume, to prepare, it will be at the midpoint. But, we know we must prepare for those four designated threats to our safety and well-being. Other events also occur at that three and a half year time, so this is most likely that time determined. How should that preparation begin?

Protect Yourself - Own A Weapon

The most expedient preparation is to own a defensive weapon. If you don't own one now, then this should be your first priority. It doesn't matter if you agree with gun ownership or not - get a weapon, unless you desire to die 'by the sword' as indicated above. You must not be naked and without defense; especially if you have a family. If you won't protect them in times of hardship; who will? If every qualified person in America owns a weapon, and our enemies know it, then we likely would never have to fire those weapons. A hostile enemy will not attack a target they know will kill them. We must let every Islamic terrorist know they will die if they attack us. Even if they have suicide bombers, they will soon run out of volunteers. But, Islamic killers are not the only great danger that might arise.

There's a serious consideration, however, before you buy that weapon. That is, to make sure you buy ammunition for it at the same time; otherwise you might own a weapon that's useless. There's a shortage of some ammunition now, and it's likely to get worse in the future. It will be easier and simpler for a despotic leader to disarm people by eliminating the availability of ammunition. Millions of weapons have been handed down from generation to generation, and are therefore unaccountable. The government has no tracer information on these weapons. Most likely, any weapon purchased within the past few years is now recorded at the new NSA center in Bluffdale, Utah. Also, be aware that any new ammunition purchases, especially with a credit card or a check, will also be recorded at that site. Don't be surprised if sometime in the future certain items may be restricted from cash purchasing. Do it now.

Also, there's another danger that lurks closer to home. It's described as 'Wormwood.' Wormwood is a great star that fell from heaven when the third angel blew the trumpet, announcing horrible things would happen. This was not a star of course, but something that affected citizens of the earth. The word condition might have been used to describe it instead of a star falling. But the word 'great' gave the condition great significance. It's an unusual event included with the other great events in this chapter, including war and natural disasters. (Revelation 8:11)

In effect, this is a description of the great impact of drugs upon our society; so great in fact that it will become a danger during the time of tribulation. The word 'wormwood' describes a family of plants that grow in the wild. The plant is mostly a source of absinthe and opiates, but one variety produces a product that's considered artificial marijuana. In general, however, it describes the increased use of drugs; so much increase that it becomes a serious danger.

Just imagine what desperate and extreme measures users might do in their attempts to get more drugs. During this time of tribulation, would they invade your home, kill everyone, then plunder your belongings to trade or sell for more drugs? Perhaps you might reconsider your disdain of owning a weapon. Perhaps you might no longer believe the arguments of those gun-haters. To comply with their ideas might get you and your family killed. Then it's too late to consider owning one. Christ cautioned many times in Revelation to be prepared; don't be caught naked. And, to be prepared means to have food, or a way to grow food.

Prepare Not to Starve

According to Revelation, and mentioned in three places, hunger will be one of the greatest hardships during the tribulation period. Each person or each family must decide how to prepare for this horrible event. One way, and of course the most obvious way, is to prepare to grow your own food during this period. This is a simple answer for farmers who have acreage and are trained in the techniques of farming.

Most farmers with large gardens also know how to can their produce for the more austere times. However, those who have no acreage or space enough to grow a garden must have other alternatives. It's uncertain if farmers can produce enough to provide for the massive hunger that will occur. Probably not; and shipping and transportation will be greatly reduced if not totally eliminated to move produce long distances. So, other options must be explored before the need arises. You must be prepared.

One option growing in popularity is to accumulate large stocks of those meals with a long life span, some up to twenty or twenty-five years. Presently, there are two major advertisers of these products, but likely there are more. For some, this is not the best option and for two reasons. First is the cost. They are more expensive than comparable meals. Second is that they require water to prepare the meal. 'Just add water and heat' the ads say. But what if you don't have water or heat?

Another reasonable alternative is to buy canned food; and it's certainly the least expensive for those on a limited budget. One might ask 'why not stock frozen food?' The answer is simple; likely there will be little or no electricity during the worst times of the tribulation. Canned food offers another great advantage. All canned foods include water and liquids in the cans. This could be one source of liquid to prevent severe thirst. Hunger and thirst are two of the four horrors described to happen during the tribulation period. But, one might be concerned about the cost, and loss through 'best by' dates on the cans.

To counter the cost of canned food one must remember the main objective during the tribulation period is survival. Therefore, quality food and the 'food you like' are not that important. The most important thing to consider is cost per unit (ounce) and 'best by' dates. For examples: most food stores and supermarkets have rotating special prices on their canned vegetables. Some cans normally priced above a dollar are put on special prices such as half that to draw customers to the store. That's the time to buy that product in quantity; as many as the store will allow. And, there's another option that might even be better; the dollar discount store.

Almost all canned food products at the 'dollar stores' are priced at a dollar. However, many of those canned items contain more than twice as much as those priced less at regular supermarkets. It's not unusual to find three times the volume at the same or lower price. In either case the 'best by' date must be considered. Since this year is 2016, the beginning stock of food should begin with dates of 2018 and beyond. Some 'best by' dates now reach as far as 2021. How much should you buy and preposition? That depends on the size of your family and those you intend to support during those trying times. It also depends on your space availability for storage. Once stored, however, those dates become important. To manage the dates, keep them stocked separately by year.

Rotation is the answer. Once you have the sufficient stock on hand then future purchases become normal purchases for the current time. And for those items nearing the 'best by' dates that haven't been used there's another good answer. Simply donate them to local food pantries and other charities that offer food to the needy. But, don't consider it a loss; instead consider it another tool of God's influence upon humans helping humans. And in some cases it might even be the source of a tax deduction.

Two other alternatives regarding a food source might also be considered. First, don't forget to have a large supply of fish hooks, fishing line, and other auxiliary fishing equipment. Fish and crustaceans are usually available in most bodies of water. Even crayfish exist is small streams. Second, powerful air rifles are now on the market for shooting small game; and some have silencers, which is an advantage if you are trying to remain safely and quietly in the background.

Have a Water Source

According to the words, during tribulation many will die from: the sword, hunger, thirst, and beasts, so one must also plan for a water source. For the many who live near a water source such as rivers, lakes, and natural springs that will not be a great problem; except possibly for the purity of the water. This problem may be countered by using a water purification system (personal ones are available for

119

about twenty dollars; often called a straw) or by boiling the water. There are also other methods of purification including the use of certain tablets. Regarding 'boiling water' perhaps this is the best place to discuss fire and heat.

Regarding a heat source, there's one that's too important to ignore. It's Revelation 7:4 which cautions against hurting the trees. Trees are also mentioned in Chapter 9; which might suggest we not destroy too many of our trees during this time of tribulation; when we are likely to be without sources of fire and heat. Can you imagine how many trees would be destroyed as a source of heat for billions of people on the earth trying to stay warm for three to seven years? Trees once were the major source of heat, but the earth had many less inhabitants. Even so, at that time many of our forests were devastated. But today there's an alternative - solar cookers and ovens.

There are several types of solar ovens, some simple and some more complex. At the present time they are somewhat expensive; the better ones in the three-hundred dollar range. However, considering their utility during difficult times that extra cost might be well worth the expense, especially if you are not in an area where wood is available; dry wood. Once a tree is cut it has to dry before it can be used for fuel. I know, because in my youth my family and many families used wood for the stove and the fireplace. We didn't have electricity until I was twelve years old.

Those solar cookers will work when there is even medium sunshine, so using them wouldn't be hassle free, but it's certainly a reasonable alternative when the sun is shining. Most, at this time, are not mass produced which means if there's a sudden demand for them they might not be available. And, there are also optional solar tubes for heating water. These are less expensive and can also be used for cooking like a stove, with the addition of an insert tray. But, what about those times when the sun isn't adequate to make those solar cookers effective? The other alternative, of course, is firewood; which likely will be the primary source for most survivors. This brings a question of how to start that fire without a match.

A large stock of matches or cigarette lighters or other fuel lighters might be the most obvious answer of how to start a fire. And, there are two alternative ways, just in case matches don't work and fuel is exhausted.

The first alternative is the camp-style striker method. There are several interpretations of the striker, where a rod is scraped against a starter producing sparks to start a fire tender. There's another alternative, however, that most people never consider. And, when the sun is shining it's definitely the most effective - the common magnifying glass. Using the sun, a magnifying glass focused to a fine point on paper or other tender will start a fire.

A very strong magnifying glass is always more effective, but a weaker magnifier will work well during the hottest times of day. The best news about the magnifying glass is that water doesn't hurt it, and the fuel never runs out. I have four strong ones pre-positioned for emergencies. Once prepared for these three threats, there's still one to consider. It's introduced as beasts, which most certainly would mean organisms, diseases, and pestilence.

Prepare for Health Disasters

If this tribulation time is as horrendous as written in the Bible, then many people will die from communicable diseases and maladies that are somewhat controllable today. Today, we have medicines and immunizations to prevent and combat things such as flu and pneumonia. Just imagine what would happen if these protections were not available for five to seven years. In large groups, these horrors would spread like wildfire, and only the healthiest and hardiest would survive, especially if complicated without heat to ease the freezing and wet nights. Without proper medications the only defense would be to wear masks and avoid large groups during these periods of epidemics. But, these maladies are not the only threats to survival.

Two other serious threats will be ticks and mosquitoes. These have been serious problems throughout history. In our modern day, and in our modern societies, repellants ordinarily repel these malicious enemies; but will repellants be available during the tribulation period? Likely not. One possibility is to try to anticipate the beginning time and have as much on hand as possible. If you have too much, your friends and family might need help. And, if you spend any time at all outdoors, especially in warmer times, always check every inch of your skin for ticks. They are very small until they gorge themselves with your blood; then it might be too late. If your home is not perfectly sealed, don't forget to sleep under netting at night.

Another common problem often arises when in survival mode; especially outdoors. That's the problem of infection from scratches and other wounds. Briars, thorns, and broken sharp sticks abound everywhere in the outdoors, even in the safety of your enclosed yard. If an infection occurs from one of these pricks, scratches, or cuts there likely will not be medical aid nearby to help you. Of course, the logical answer to defend yourself against these 'beasts' is to have an adequate stock of antiseptics and antibiotics on hand to last the duration. These beasts will kill people as surely as guns, hunger, and thirst; and often with long-lasting pain.

In conclusion, the stage for this tribulation period has already been set. That happened with the signing of that covenant that will cause many disasters and horrors at that time of tribulation 'in the midst' of the covenant time agreement. Will it really matter which candidate is elected this November if the tribulation begins soon thereafter? Only time will tell, but we will surely need a leader guided by honesty and integrity to guide us through that time of horrors. Can Hillary Clinton be trusted to guide us back to the path toward God's love and guidance? I think not. She has already invited Satan into our house.

This is my analysis and interpretation of current events in relationship to the Words in Revelation. Am I worthy to make these interpretations? I hope. Am I writing this hoping for true guidance from God? In God's name I pray that is so.

God bless America, and protect Israel

About the Author

Will Clark's author experiences began by writing inspection and evaluation reports in the U.S. Air Force. He is a retired Air Force officer and a Vietnam veteran, serving in Saigon from 1966 to 1967. His other overseas assignments include Misawa, Japan and Ankara, Turkey; where he visited the ancient sites of the Seven Churches.

In 1995, as a 'Friends of Education' study skills project, he authored a book, *How to Learn*, to encourage students to improve their grades in DeSoto County, Mississippi. Education supporters printed and distributed four thousand copies. The following school year he wrote a weekly education column for a local newspaper, *The DeSoto County Tribune*. He also taught an adult GED class. His book, *How to Learn*, has been updated and is now available everywhere.

His next published book was *School Bells and Broken Tales*, a parody of nursery rhyme characters, also a motivation and education book for children. Other books include *Shades of Retribution,* a historical novel, and *Simply Success*, a motivation guide for students and employees.

His action novel, The Atlantis Crystal, is the first of a trilogy based on Atlantis and crystals. The other two books are: *She Waits in Atlantis*, and *Return to Atlantis*. This trilogy is based on his travels while assigned to Turkey, site of the ancient city of Troy. His latest political thriller is: *America 20XX: The New World Order.*

The past five years he has devoted his full time to the study, research, and writing of an analysis of the Book of Revelation and the danger of Satan, that beast that guides Islam.

Things We Must Never Forget

Benghazi

Why were four Americans killed?
Where was Hillary Clinton while it was happening?
Where was Barack Obama while it was happening?
Why did they lie and blame the event on a video?
Why were rescuers on 'stand by' told to 'stand down?'

Fast and Furious

Who authorized the operation?
Why did the operation continue after weapons were lost?
Why did the procedure have no procedure?
Why weren't tracking devices used?

The IRS Scandal

What was the highest level involved?
Who initiated it?
Why hasn't anyone been fired or reprimanded?
What dangers could be unleashed by this organization?

Greatest Quotes
of Our Time

Michelle Obama

February 18, 2008
"For the first time in my adult life I am proud of my country."
(Age 44)

Barack Obama

March 9, 2008"We are no longer a Christian nation - at least not just."
September 25, 2012
Remarks to the UN General Assembly
"The future must not belong to those who slander Islam."

Nancy Pelosi

March 9, 2010
"We have to pass the bill so that you can find out what is in it."

Hillary Clinton

January 23, 2013
"What difference, at this point, does it make?"

December 3, 2014
"...showing respect even for one's enemies, trying to understand and insofar as psychologically possible, empathize with their perspective and point of view."

Other Books by the Author

Novels

Shades of Retribution
The Atlantis Crystal
She Waits in Atlantis
Return to Atlantis
America 20XX: The New World Order
666: Mark of the Beast
Death Drones: 2025

Children's Books:

Forest Trails and Fairy Tales
Wishing Wells and Broken Tales
Student Study Skills
American Heroes: Students Who Learn

Non-Fiction:

Obama, Hillary, Saul Alinsky and their Useful Idiots
Simply Success
The Education Jungle
How to Learn
The Day America Died
Obama's Ring: The Seat of Satan
Managing Without Conflict
The Peer Pressure Monster
Denied 3 Times
The War on Christians
Who is the Antichrist

Islamic Two-Headed Beast
Islam Attacks the Whore
The Second Beast
Secrets of the Seven Churches
Two Woman of the Apocalypse
Islam's Bloodthirsty Sword
Once Upon A Revelation: About Islam
America Gasps
God's Islamaknowbe Warriors
Who is the Antichrist Beast?
Who is the False Prophet Beast?
Who is the Woman Jezebel?
Who is Babylon the Great?
What is the Tribulation